I0434814

United States
Department of
Agriculture

Forest Service

**Northern
Research Station**

Resource Bulletin
NRS-71

Assessing Urban Forest Effects and Values of the Great Plains: Kansas, Nebraska, North Dakota, South Dakota

David J. Nowak
Robert E. Hoehn III
Daniel E. Crane
Allison R. Bodine

Abstract

This report details the evaluation of the urban tree resources of the north-central Great Plains region of the United States. Specifically this report provides a more comprehensive understanding of the species composition and structural and functional benefits of the urban forests in the states of Kansas (33.1 million urban trees), Nebraska (13.3 million urban trees), North Dakota (975,000 urban trees), and South Dakota (5.4 million urban trees). Information on the structure and functions of the urban forest can be used to inform urban forest management programs and to integrate urban forests within plans to improve environmental quality throughout the Great Plains region. The results are reported for each state and may be accessed at: http://www.nrs.fs.fed.us/data/urban.

Acknowledgments

Our thanks go to: in **Kansas** - Tim McDonnell, Community Forestry Program Leader and Robert Atchison, Rural Forestry Program Leader; in **Nebraska** - Eric Berg, Community Forests & Sustainable Landscapes Program Leader and Steve Rasmussen, GPI Coordinator/ District Forester; in **North Dakota** - Thomas Claeys, Forestry and Fire Management Team Leader; in **South Dakota** - Coe Foss, Forest Health Program Supervisor, Chris Johnson, Community Forestry Coordinator, and Tiffany Arp, Community Forestry Coordinator for their help with this project and review of the report. We also thank the field data collectors in North Dakota - Sharon Bartels, Trent Bristol, Lorin Fornes, Robert Harsel, Gerri Makay, Joel Nichols , Sarah Tunge, and the summer intern/inventory crews in Kansas, Nebraska, and South Dakota.

Cover Photo

Elms along University Avenue, Fargo, ND. Wikimedia Commons.

Assessing Urban Forest Effects and Values of the Great Plains: Kansas, Nebraska, North Dakota, South Dakota

David J. Nowak
Robert E. Hoehn III
Daniel E. Crane
Allison R. Bodine

The Authors

DAVID J. NOWAK is a research forester and project leader with the U.S. Forest Service's Northern Research Station at Syracuse, New York.

ROBERT E. HOEHN III is a forester with the U.S. Forest Service's Northern Research Station at Syracuse, New York.

DANIEL E. CRANE is an information technology specialist with the U.S. Forest Service's Northern Research Station at Syracuse, New York.

ALLISON R. BODINE is a research forester with the Davey Institute at Syracuse, New York.

CONTENTS

Introduction   1

Kansas' Urban Forest   7

Nebraska's Urban Forest   17

North Dakota's Urban Forest   27

South Dakota's Urban Forest   37

Conclusion   46

References   47

Appendix I   52

Appendix II   54

Appendix III   59

Appendix IV   64

Appendix V   69

Appendix VI   74

Appendix VII   75

INTRODUCTION

The north-central Great Plains of the United States is unique in character as well as the challenges it faces. The vastness of open plains with its extreme heat or cold, windy conditions, and unpredictable precipitation throughout the year can make for uncomfortable living in the region. Trees are a very important and valued component in the landscape around homes and communities. They help buffer the weather conditions, conserve energy, attract wildlife, reduce air pollution, limit soil erosion, lower storm water runoff, and produce many other benefits to individual homeowners and communities in the region. These benefits can be enhanced through proactive tree planting and management strategies which encompass and engage the community.

Urban and community forests comprise all trees, both within and outside forested stands, which occur within urban and community areas. Urban areas are defined by the U.S. Census Bureau definition of urbanized areas and urban clusters. Community land is delimited based on jurisdictional or political boundaries delimited by U.S. Census Bureau definitions of incorporated or designated places. The union of these two areas determines the urban and community forests (hereafter referred to collectively as urban forest) within the states. In some states (e.g., South Dakota), community areas were excluded as they were considered to be rural lands by state personnel on the project (e.g., large reservations).

The urban forest resources include all trees within the urban boundaries—boulevard trees, trees planted within city parks, and trees that naturally occur within city limits or public rights-of-way. This urban forest also includes trees that are planted or naturally regenerate on private or commercial properties. The management of urban tree resources may often fall under the responsibility of city foresters, public works departments, private citizens, and/or community tree boards.

In an effort to analyze the value of trees in the north-central Great Plains region, the state forestry agencies of Kansas, Nebraska, North Dakota, and South Dakota have collaborated on a project to inventory and evaluate the rural and urban tree resources across the four states. With help from the Western Forestry Leadership Coalition, the states submitted the "Great Plains Tree and Forest Invasives Initiative" (GPI) as a U.S. Forest Service (USFS) State and Private Forestry National Redesign Pilot Project for funding in 2007. The primary objectives of the project were to develop a multi-state, regional approach to sample nonforest area trees (areas not sampled by the Forest Service Forest Inventory and Analysis [FIA] program), to gain a better understanding of species composition and tree health conditions and benefits, and to prepare for and address invasive tree pests such emerald ash borer.

Analysis of 1,213 rural plots across the four states was performed by the USFS National Inventory and Monitoring Applications Center (NIMAC). Analysis of data from 887 urban and community plots (188 plots in Kansas, 200 plots in Nebraska, 299 plots in North Dakota, and 200 plots in South Dakota) was performed by the U.S. Forest Service, Northern Research Station, using the i-Tree Eco model.[1] This report summarizes these results and values of the region and individual state urban forests':

- Structure
- Potential risk to from insects or diseases
- Air pollution removal
- Carbon storage
- Annual carbon removal (sequestration)
- Changes in building energy use

The results of these analyses supersede estimates of urban forests provided in the publication Urban and Community Forests of the North Central West Region[2], which was based on the 2001 National Land Cover Database (NLCD) estimates. The data in this report provide more timely and accurate estimates for the four states as they are based on locally derived field data.

i-Tree Eco Model and Field Measurements

To help determine the vegetation structure, functions, and values of the urban trees in Kansas, Nebraska, North Dakota, and South Dakota, a vegetation assessment was conducted during the summers of 2008 and 2009. For this assessment, 0.167-acre field plots (a total of 887 plots) were sampled and analyzed using the i-Tree Eco model.[1]

i-Tree Eco is designed to use standardized field data from randomly located plots and local hourly air pollution and meteorological data to quantify urban forest structure and its numerous effects, including:

- Urban forest structure (e.g., species composition, tree density, tree health, leaf area, leaf and tree biomass, species diversity, etc.).
- Amount of pollution removed hourly by the urban forest and its associated percent air quality improvement throughout a year. Pollution removal is calculated for ozone, sulfur dioxide, nitrogen dioxide, carbon monoxide, and particulate matter (<10 microns).
- Total carbon stored and net carbon annually sequestered by the urban forest.
- Effects of trees on building energy use and consequent effects on carbon dioxide emissions from power plants.
- Compensatory value of the forest, as well as the value of air pollution removal and carbon storage and sequestration.
- Potential impact of infestations by Asian longhorned beetle, emerald ash borer, gypsy moth, or Dutch elm disease.

For more information go to www.itreetools.org

In 2008 and 2009, funding was received to conduct an inventory and vegetation assessment of the urban forest resources across the four states. Data collection in 2008 was carried out by field crews of summer employees supervised by state forestry personnel in Kansas, Nebraska, and South Dakota, and existing state forestry staff in North Dakota. Most of the plots were visited by two-person crews with some North Dakota plots being visited by a single staff person. North Dakota evaluated additional rural and urban plots in 2009 utilizing the same personnel. In both years, most of the data collection occurred between mid-May and the end of August.

Field data collection took place during the leaf-on season to properly assess tree canopies. Within each plot, data included land use, tree cover, and individual tree attributes of species, stem-diameter at breast height (d.b.h.; measured at 4.5 ft), tree height, height to base of live crown, crown width, percentage crown canopy missing and dieback, and distance and direction to residential buildings.[3] Trees were recorded as woody plants with a diameter greater than or equal to 1 inch d.b.h. As many species are classified as small tree/large shrub, the 1-inch minimum d.b.h. of all species means that many species commonly considered shrubs will be included in the species tallies when they meet the minimum diameter requirement.

During field data collection, trees sampled in the inventoried plots were classified by genus, though some trees were indentified to the species level. In the event that a tree was identified to the species level (e.g., Siberian elm) and other trees of the same genus were sampled, the genera classification (e.g., elm) includes all sampled trees of the genus that could not be classified to a specific species level. Trees designated as "hardwood" or "softwood" include the sampled trees that could not be identified as a more specific species or genera classification. Since hardwood and softwood are species groups that comprise multiple species and genera, they are not included in the analysis of the most common species. In this report, tree species, genera, or species groups are hereafter referred to as tree species.

To calculate carbon storage, biomass for each tree was estimated using equations from the literature and measured tree data. Open-grown, maintained trees tend to have less biomass than predicted by forest-derived biomass equations.[4] To adjust for this difference, biomass results for open-grown urban trees are multiplied by 0.8.[4] No adjustment was made for trees found in natural stand conditions. Tree dry-weight biomass was converted to stored carbon by multiplying by 0.5.[4]

To estimate the gross amount of carbon sequestered annually, average diameter growth from appropriate genera and diameter class and tree condition was added to the existing tree diameter (year x) to estimate tree diameter and carbon storage in year $x+1$.

Air pollution removal estimates are derived from calculated hourly tree-canopy resistances for ozone and sulfur and nitrogen dioxides based on a hybrid of big-leaf and multi-layer canopy deposition models.[5,6] As the removal of carbon monoxide and particulate matter by vegetation is not directly related to transpiration, removal rates (deposition velocities) for these pollutants were based on average measured values from the literature[7,8] that were adjusted depending on leaf phenology and leaf area. Particulate removal incorporated a 50 percent resuspension rate of particles back to the atmosphere.[9]

Seasonal effects of trees on residential building energy use was calculated based on procedures described in the literature[10] using distance and direction of trees from residential structures, tree height, and tree condition data.

Compensatory values were based on valuation procedures of the Council of Tree and Landscape Appraisers[11], which uses tree species, diameter, condition, and location information.[12]

To learn more about i-Tree Eco methods[12] visit: http://nrs.fs.fed.us/tools/ufore/ or www. itreetools.org.

Great Plains' Urban Forest Resource

The plots in Kansas, Nebraska, and South Dakota were categorized as the following land uses: residential and multi-family, commercial/institutional/transportation, agriculture, and "other" land uses. North Dakota plots were classified as residential and multi-family, commercial/institutional, agriculture, "other," and transportation land uses. The most prevalent land use was residential and multi-family in Kansas, Nebraska, and South Dakota, and agriculture in North Dakota (Table 1).

Table 1.—Urban land use distribution by state

State	Land Use	% Area[a]
Kansas	Residential/ Multi-Family	32.2
	Commercial/Institutional/Transportation	26.3
	Agriculture	22.2
	Other	19.2
Nebraska	Residential/ Multi-Family	44.5
	Commercial/Institutional/Transportation	24.0
	Other	17.0
	Agriculture	14.5
North Dakota	Agriculture	30.1
	Residential/Multi-Family	25.4
	Other	18.4
	Commercial/Institutional	17.4
	Transportation	8.7
South Dakota	Residential/Multifamily/Farms	28.8
	Other	27.3
	Commercial/Institutional/Transport	24.7
	Agriculture	19.2

[a] The percentage of the total urban land area within the state

An analysis of the collected data shows that the north-central Great Plains regional urban forest has an estimated 52.8 million trees. Tree cover in each state was estimated based on photo interpretation of Google™ imagery or cover estimates from field plot data.[13] The greatest percentage of urban tree cover was found in South Dakota (17.0 percent), followed by Nebraska (15.0 percent), Kansas (14.0 percent), and North Dakota (2.7 percent). Elm was the only tree species found among the top five most common species in all four states (Table 2).

Trees in the north-central Great Plains regional urban forest remove an estimated 14,471 tons of air pollution per year ($105.3 million per year). Pollution removal is highest in Nebraska (6,714 tons/yr), followed by Kansas (6,256 tons/yr), South Dakota (1,350 tons/yr), and North Dakota (151 tons/yr). Additionally, Great Plains trees are estimated to reduce annual residential energy costs by $51.7 million per year based on local 2007 energy costs.[14] Reduced annual residential energy costs are greatest in Nebraska ($28.2 million per year), followed by Kansas ($19.7 million per year), North Dakota ($3.3 million per year), and South Dakota ($519,000 per year; Table 3).

Table 2.—Five most common urban tree species by state

State	Common Name	% Population[a]
Kansas	Elm	15.4
	Hackberry	10.1
	Juniper	8.0
	Maple	6.8
	Walnut	5.5
Nebraska	Hackberry	14.9
	Mulberry	12.6
	Siberian elm	11.4
	Juniper	10.7
	Elm	8.6
North Dakota	Ash	38.5
	Spruce	13.4
	Boxelder	8.6
	Eastern cottonwood	8.0
	Elm	6.4
South Dakota	Ponderosa pine	21.3
	Ash	20.4
	Willow	9.3
	Pine	8.3
	Elm	5.7

[a] The percentage of the total tree population within the state

The following sections provide more detailed findings for each state.

Table 3.—North-central Great Plains urban forest summary

	Kansas	Nebraska	North Dakota	South Dakota
Number of trees	33,141,000	13,317,000	975,000	5,414,000
Tree cover (%)	14.0	15.0	2.7	17.0
Pollution removal				
tons[a]/year	6,256	6,714	151	1,350
$ million/year	47.4	46.8	1.1	10.0
Carbon storage				
tons[a]	4,400,000	2,100,000	243,000	697,000
$ million	91.9	43.4	5.0	14.4
Carbon sequestration				
tons[a]/year	169,600	84,500	8,800	28,400
$ per year	3,500,000	1,700,000	182,000	588,000
Building energy reduction				
$ per year	19,700,000	28,200,000	3,300,000	519,000
Reduced carbon emissions				
$ per year	780,000	1,000,000	157,000	7,300
Compensatory value				
$ billion	18.1	9.8	1.3	5.1

[a] Ton – short ton (U.S.) (2,000 lbs)

Introduction

Urban and community forests are highly valued in the Great Plains. An urban or community forest (hereafter referred to as urban forest) refers to the collection of trees, shrubs, and related vegetation growing in cities and towns. These areas include city parks, streetscapes, and trees on public, private, and commercial lands. A large and diverse number of tree species are found in urban and community areas, with the typical Kansas urban forest dominated by elm, hackberry, juniper, maple, and walnut species.

Based on 2000 U.S. Census data, Kansas has a population of 2.7 million people, of which 83.4 percent reside within urban or community areas (areas delimited by census defined incorporated or designated places).[15] The trees and forests in all of these municipalities provide a range of valuable environmental, social, and economic benefits. For every dollar that is invested in the urban forest resource, there is typically a positive net annual benefit over the lifespan of a publically owned municipal tree.[16] Many of the urban and community areas in Kansas rely on state programs, funding, and forestry professionals to maintain healthy urban forest resources. This report provides a platform to further develop urban forest management programs. For more information on the forestry programs and services provided by the state of Kansas, please refer to Appendix I.

To help assess Kansas' urban forest, data from 188 field plots located throughout the State were analyzed using the Forest Service's i-Tree Eco model.[1] Field data were collected by summer intern/inventory crews. In the field, 1/6-acre plots were selected based on a random sample with an average density of approximately one plot for every 5,096 acres. The randomly selected plots were categorized to the following land uses: residential and multi-family (60 plots, 32.3 percent of area); commercial/institutional/transportation (50 plots, 26.3 percent); agriculture (44 plots, 22.2 percent); and "other" (34 plots, 19.2 percent; Fig 1).

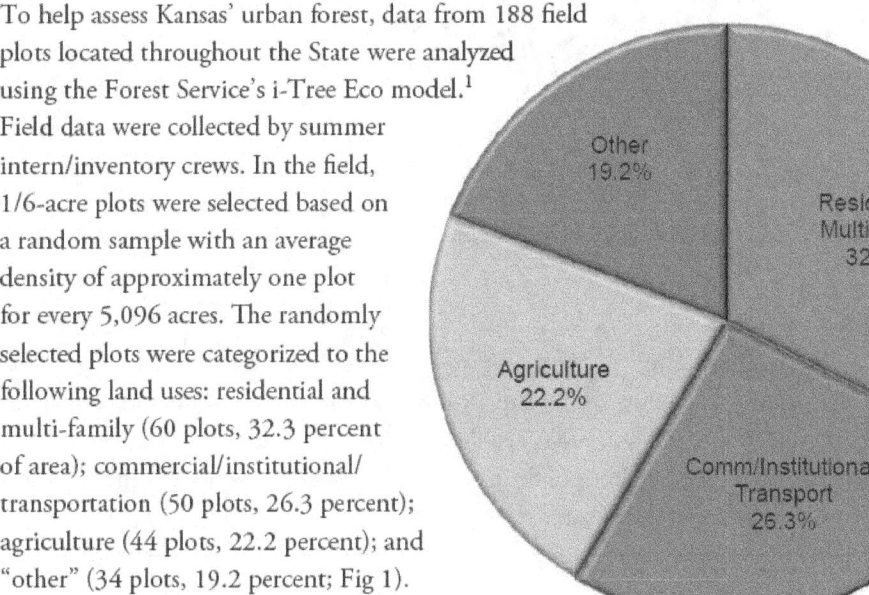

Figure 1.—Land-use distribution, Kansas, 2008, for inventoried plots.

Tree Characteristics of the Urban Forest

Kansas has an estimated 33,141,000 urban trees (standard error [SE] of 5,313,000). Urban tree cover in Kansas is estimated to be 14.0 percent.[13] The five most common species[a] in the urban forest were elm (15.4 percent), hackberry (10.1 percent), juniper (8.0 percent), maple (6.8 percent), and walnut (5.5 percent). The 10 most common species account for 69.3 percent of all trees; their relative abundance is illustrated in Figure 2. Twenty-six different tree species were sampled in Kansas; these species and their relative abundance and distribution by land use are presented in Appendix II.

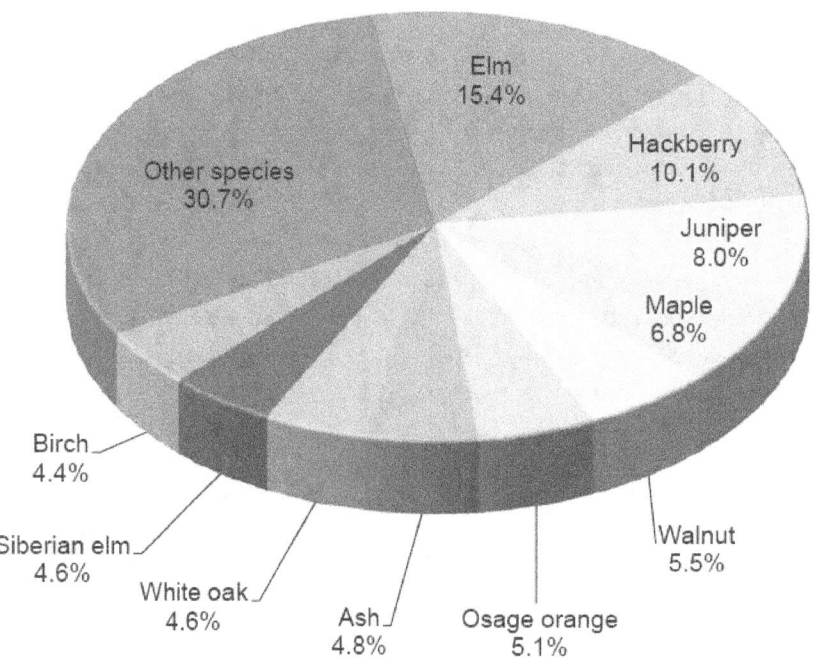

Figure 2.—Urban tree species composition, Kansas, 2008.

The highest density of trees occurs in "other" land uses (92.8 trees per acre), followed by residential and multi-family land (33.0 trees per acre) (Fig. 3.) The overall urban tree density in Kansas is 34.6 trees per acre, which is relatively low compared to other states' tree densities that range between 3.8 and 182.3 trees per acre (Appendix VI). Trees with diameters less than 6 inches account for 66.1 percent of the population (Figs. 4, 5). Land uses that contain the most leaf area are residential and multi-family lands (46.9 percent of total tree leaf area) and "other" (39.0 percent).

---

[a] During field data collection, trees sampled in the inventoried plots were classified by genus, though some trees were indentified to the species level. In the event that a tree was identified to the species level (e.g., Siberian elm) and other trees of the same genus were sampled, the genera classification (e.g., elm) includes all sampled trees of the genus that could not be classified to a specific species level. Trees designated as "hardwood" or "softwood" include the sampled trees that could not be identified as a more specific species or genera classification. Since hardwood and softwood are species groups that comprise multiple species and genera, they are not included in the analysis of the most common species. In this report, tree species, genera, or species groups are hereafter referred to as tree species.

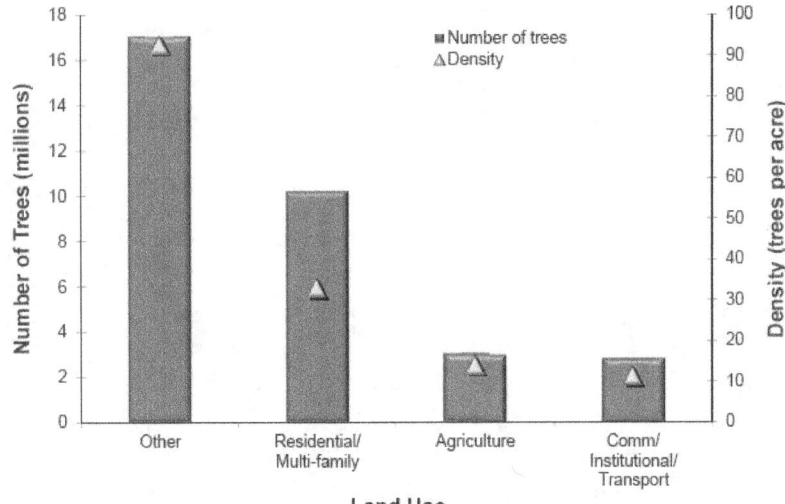

Figure 3.—Number of urban trees and tree density by land use, Kansas, 2008.

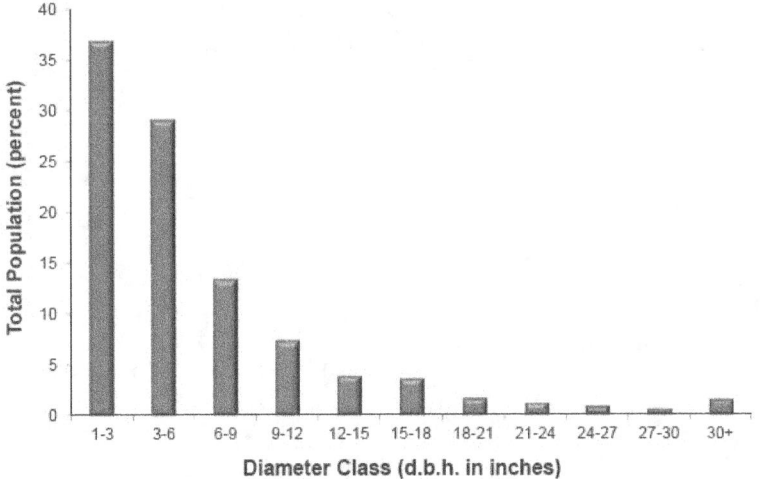

Figure 4.—Percent of total population by diameter class, Kansas, 2008.

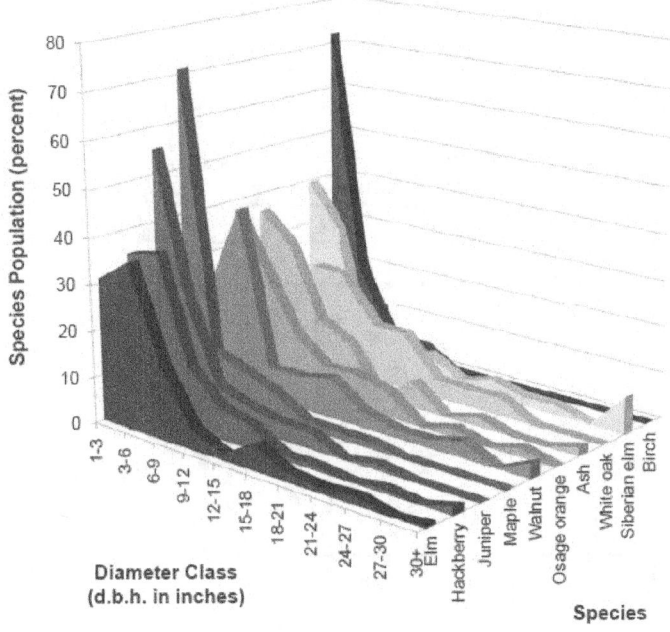

Figure 5.—Percent of species population by diameter class for 10 most common tree species, Kansas, 2008.

Urban Forest Leaf Area

Many tree benefits are linked to the healthy leaf surface area of the plant, i.e. the greater the leaf area, the greater the benefit. In Kansas, tree species with the greatest leaf area are elm, hackberry, and walnut (Fig. 6).

Tree species with relatively large individuals contributing leaf area to the population (species with percent of leaf area much greater than percent of total population) are silver maple, eastern cottonwood, and walnut. Tree species with smaller individuals in the population are birch, honeylocust, and mulberry (species with percent of leaf area much less than percentage of total population). The species must also have constituted at least 1 percent of the total population to be considered as relatively large or small trees in the population.

Importance values (IV) are calculated using a formula that takes into account the relative leaf area and relative abundance. High importance values do not mean that these trees should necessarily be planted in the future, rather these species currently dominate the urban forest structure. The species in the urban forest with the greatest IVs are elm, hackberry, and walnut (Table 4).

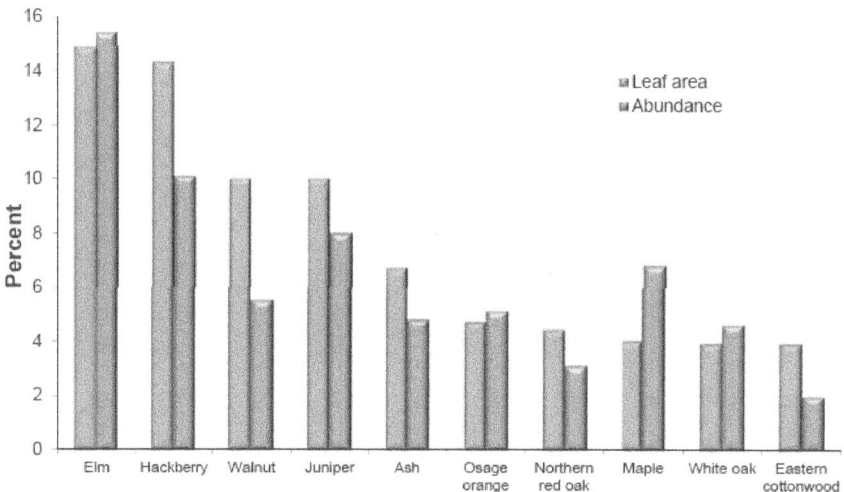

Figure 6.—Percent of total population (abundance) and leaf area for 10 most common tree species, Kansas, 2008.

Table 4.—Percent of total population, percent of total leaf area, and importance values of species with the greatest importance values, Kansas, 2008

Common Name	%Pop[a]	%LA[b]	IV[c]
Elm	15.4	14.9	30.3
Hackberry	10.1	14.3	24.4
Walnut	5.5	10.0	15.5
Juniper	8.0	6.7	14.7
Maple	6.8	3.9	10.7
Osage orange	5.1	4.4	9.5
Ash	4.8	4.7	9.5
White oak	4.6	3.9	8.5
Siberian elm	4.6	3.6	8.2
Northern red oak	3.1	4.0	7.1

[a] %Pop – percent of total tree population
[b] %LA – percent of total leaf area
[c] IV = %Pop + %LA

Air Pollution Removal by Urban Trees

Poor air quality is a common problem in many urban areas and can lead to human health problems, damage to landscape materials and ecosystem processes, and reduced visibility. The urban forest can help improve air quality by reducing air temperature, directly removing pollutants from the air, and reducing energy consumption in buildings, which consequently reduces air pollutant emissions from power plants. Trees also emit volatile organic compounds that can contribute to ozone formation. However, integrative studies have revealed that an increase in tree cover leads to reduced ozone formation.[17]

Pollution removal by trees in Kansas was estimated using the i-Tree Eco model in conjunction with field data and hourly pollution and weather data for the year 2000. Pollution removal was greatest for ozone (O_3), followed by particulate matter less than 10 microns (PM_{10}), sulfur dioxide (SO_2), nitrogen dioxide (NO_2), and carbon monoxide (CO) (Fig. 7). It is estimated that trees remove 6,256 tons of air pollution (CO, NO_2, O_3, PM_{10}, SO_2) per year with an associated value of $47.4 million (based on estimated 2007 national median externality costs associated with pollutants[18]). General urban forestry management recommendations to improve air quality are given in Appendix IV.

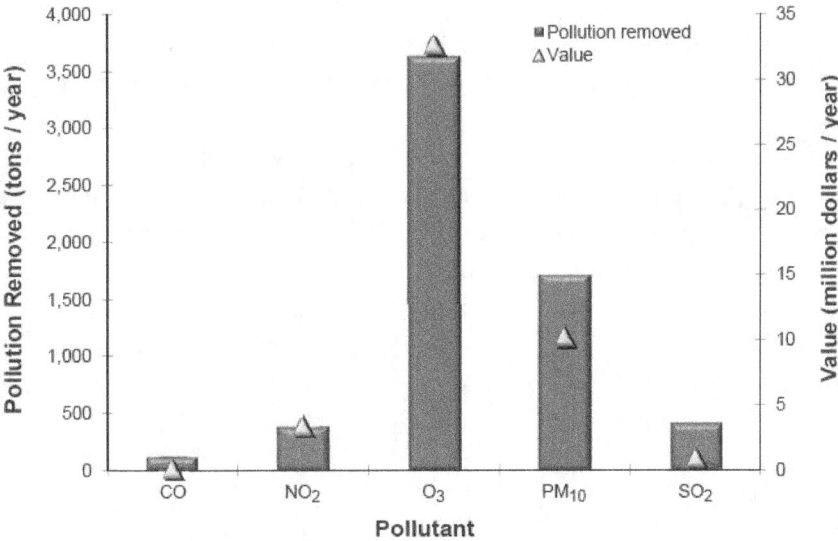

Figure 7.—Annual air pollution removal and value by urban trees, Kansas, 2008.

Carbon Storage and Sequestration

Climate change is an issue of global concern to many. Urban trees can help mitigate climate change by sequestering atmospheric carbon (from carbon dioxide) in tissue and by reducing energy use in buildings, thus reducing carbon dioxide emissions from fossil-fuel based power plants.[19]

Trees reduce the amount of carbon in the atmosphere by sequestering carbon in new tissue growth. The amount of carbon annually sequestered is increased with healthier and larger diameter trees. Gross sequestration by urban trees in Kansas is about 169,600 tons of carbon per year (621,800 tons per year of carbon dioxide) with an associated value of $3.5 million per year (Fig. 8). Net carbon sequestration in Kansas is estimated at about 131,900 tons per year (483,700 tons per year of carbon dioxide) based on estimated carbon loss due to tree mortality and decomposition.

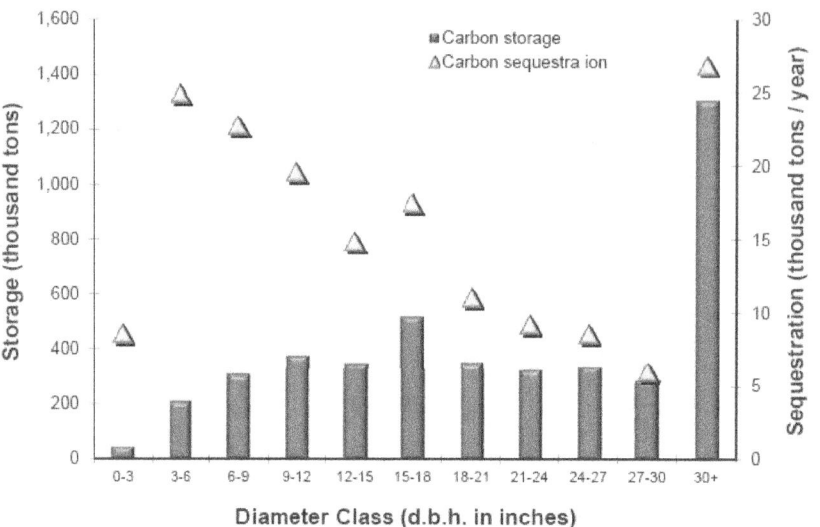

Figure 8.—Total carbon storage and sequestration by diameter class, Kansas, 2008.

Carbon storage by trees is another way trees can influence global climate change. As trees grow, they store more carbon by holding it in their accumulated tissue. As trees die and decay, they release much of the stored carbon back into the atmosphere. Thus, carbon storage is an indication of the amount of carbon that can be released if trees are allowed to die and decompose. Maintaining healthy trees will keep the carbon stored in trees, but tree maintenance can contribute to carbon emissions.[20] When trees die, utilizing the wood in long-term wood products or to heat buildings or produce energy will help reduce carbon emissions from wood decomposition or from fossil-fuel based power plants. Trees in Kansas store an estimated 4.4 million tons of carbon (16.3 million tons of carbon dioxide) ($91.9 million). Of all the species sampled, elm stores the most carbon (approximately 12.1 percent of total carbon stored) and annually sequesters the most carbon (13.8 percent of all sequestered carbon; Fig. 9).

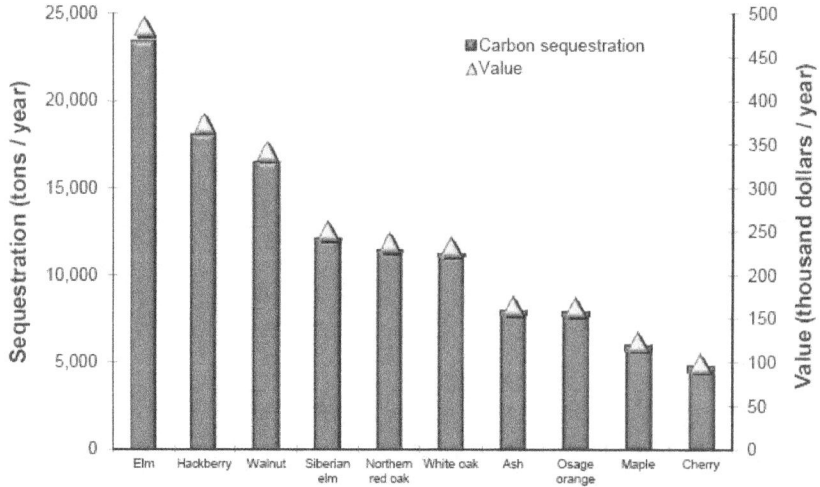

Figure 9.—Annual carbon sequestration and value for urban tree species with the greatest sequestration, Kansas, 2008.

Trees Affect Energy Use in Buildings

Trees affect energy consumption by shading buildings, providing evaporative cooling, and blocking winter winds. Trees tend to reduce building energy consumption in the summer months and can either increase or decrease building energy use in the winter months, depending on the location of trees around the building. To enhance or sustain evaporative cooling from trees in Kansas, many trees are or may need to be irrigated. Estimates of tree effects on energy use are based on field measurements of tree distance and direction to space-conditioned residential buildings.[10]

Based on average energy costs in 2007, trees in Kansas reduce energy costs from residential buildings by an estimated $19.7 million annually (Tables 5, 6). Trees also provide an additional $780,000 in value per year by reducing the amount of carbon released by fossil-fuel based power plants (a reduction of 37,700 tons of carbon emissions or 138,200 tons of carbon dioxide).

Table 5.—Annual energy savings (MBTU, MWH, and tons) due to trees near residential buildings, Kansas, 2008

	Heating	Cooling	Total
MBTU[a]	843,200	n/a	843,200
MWH[b]	4,800	93,400	98,200
Carbon avoided (t)	16,000	21,700	37,700

[a]MBTU – Million British Thermal Units
[b]MWH – Megawatt-hour

Table 6.—Annual monetary savings[c] (dollars) in residential energy expenditures during heating and cooling seasons, Kansas, 2008

	Heating	Cooling	Total
MBTU[a]	$11,611,000	n/a	11,611,000
MWH[b]	395,000	7,711,000	8,106,000
Carbon avoided	331,000	449,000	780,000

[a]MBTU – Million British Thermal Units
[b]MWH – Megawatt-hour
[c]Based on 2007 statewide energy costs[13]

Structural and Functional Values

Urban forests have a structural value based on the tree itself, which includes a compensatory value[11] (e.g., the cost of having to replace the tree with a similar tree) and the value of the carbon stored in the tree. The compensatory value of the trees and forests in Kansas is about $18.1 billion and the carbon storage of Kansas trees is estimated at $91.9 million (Fig. 10). The structural value of an urban forest tends to increase with an increase in the number and size of healthy trees.

Urban forests also have functional values (either positive or negative) based on the functions the tree performs. Functional values also tend to increase with increased number and size of healthy trees and are usually on the order of several million dollars per year. There are many other functional values of the urban forest, though they are not quantified here (e.g., reduction in air temperatures and ultraviolet radiation, improvements in water quality,

aesthetics, wildlife habitat, etc.). Through proper management, urban forest values can be increased. However, the values and benefits can also decrease as the amount of healthy tree cover declines.

Urban trees in Kansas have the following structural values:

- Compensatory value = $18.1 billion
- Carbon storage = $91.9 million

Urban trees in Kansas have the following annual functional values:

- Carbon sequestration = $3.5 million
- Pollution removal = $47.4 million
- Reduced energy costs = $19.7 million

More detailed information on the urban trees and forests in Kansas can be found at http://nrs.fs.fed.us/data/urban. Additionally, information on other urban forest values and tree statistics by diameter class can be found in Appendix II.

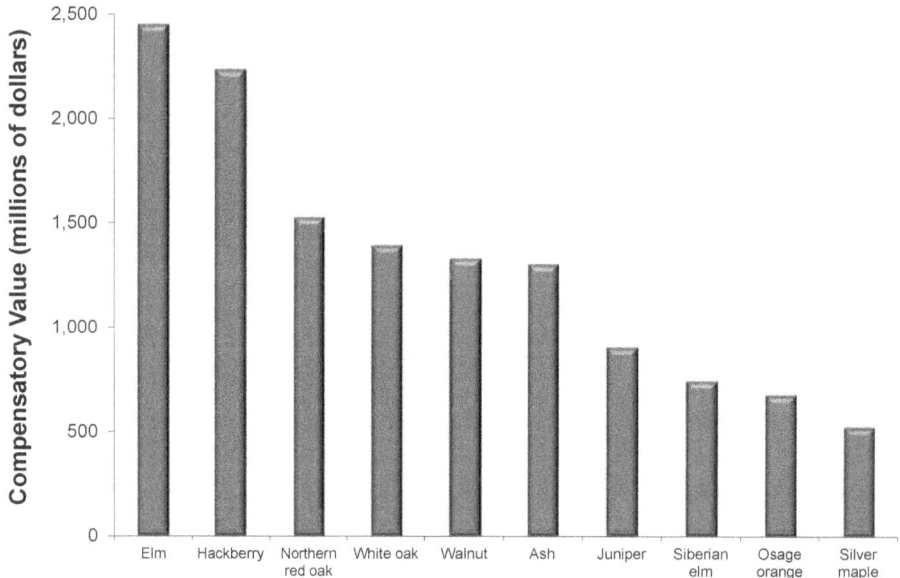

Figure 10.—Tree species with the greatest compensatory value, Kansas, 2008. Total compensatory value for all trees is $18.1 billion.

Potential Insect and Disease Impacts

Various insects and diseases can infest urban forests, potentially killing trees and reducing the health, value, and sustainability of the urban forest. Various pests have different tree hosts, so the potential damage or risk of each pest will differ. Four exotic pests/diseases were analyzed for their potential impact: Asian longhorned beetle, gypsy moth, emerald ash borer, and Dutch elm disease (Fig. 11). Lists of hosts for these pests/diseases can be found at http://nrs.fs.fed.us/tools/ufore/.

The Asian longhorned beetle (ALB)[21] is an insect that bores into and kills a wide range of hardwood species. This beetle was discovered in 1996 in Brooklyn, NY, and has subsequently spread to Long Island, Queens, and Manhattan. In 1998, the beetle was discovered in the suburbs of Chicago, IL. Beetles have also been found in Jersey City, NJ (2002), Toronto/Vaughan, Ontario (2003), and Middlesex/Union counties, NJ (2004). In 2007, the beetle was found on Staten and Prall's Island, NY. Most recently, beetles were detected in Worcester, MA (2008). This beetle represents a potential loss to Kansas of $7.1 billion in compensatory value (45.8 percent of live tree population).

Gypsy moth (GM)[22] is a defoliator that feeds on many species causing widespread defoliation and tree death if outbreak conditions last several years. This pest could potentially result in damage to or a loss of $3.5 billion in compensatory value of Kansas's urban trees (10.6 percent of live tree population).

Since being discovered in Detroit in 2002, emerald ash borer (EAB)[23] has killed millions of ash trees in Illinois, Indiana, Iowa, Kentucky, Maryland, Michigan, Minnesota, Missouri, New York, Ohio, Ontario, Pennsylvania, Quebec, Tennessee, Virginia, West Virginia, and Wisconsin. EAB has the potential to affect 4.7 percent of Kansas's urban tree population ($1.3 billion in compensatory value).

American elm, one of the most important street trees in the 20th century, has been devastated by the Dutch elm disease (DED). Since first reported in the 1930s, it has killed more than 50 percent of the native elm population in the United States.[24] Although some elm species have shown varying degrees of resistance, Kansas possibly could lose 15.5 percent of its trees to this disease ($2.5 billion in compensatory value).

More information on trees in Kansas can be found at: http://nrs.fs.fed.us/data/urban.

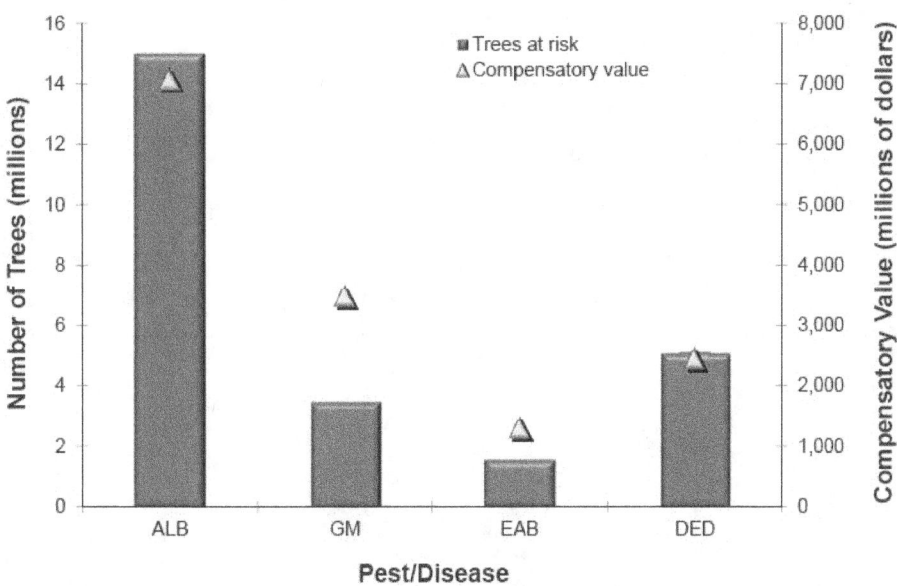

Figure 11.—Number of trees at risk and potential compensatory value of pest/disease effects, Kansas, 2008.

Nebraska Forest Service

Introduction

Urban and community forests are highly valued in the Great Plains. An urban or community forest (hereafter referred to as urban forest) refers to the collection of trees, shrubs, and related vegetation growing in cities and towns. These areas include city parks, streetscapes, and trees on public, private, and commercial lands. A large and diverse number of tree species are found in urban and community areas, with the typical Nebraska urban forest dominated by hackberry, mulberry, Siberian elm, juniper, and other elm species.

Based on 2000 U.S. Census data, Nebraska has a population of 1.7 million people, of which 83.3 percent reside within urban or community areas (areas delimited by census defined incorporated or designated places).[15] The trees and forests in all of these municipalities provide a range of valuable environmental, social, and economic benefits. For every dollar that is invested in the urban forest resource there is typically a positive net annual benefit over the lifespan of a publically owned municipal tree.[16] Many of the urban and community areas in Nebraska rely on state programs, funding, and forestry professionals to maintain healthy urban forest resources. This report provides a platform to further develop urban forest management programs. For more information on the forestry programs and services provided by the state of Nebraska, please refer to Appendix I.

To help assess Nebraska's urban forest, data from 200 field plots located throughout the State were analyzed using the Forest Service's i-Tree Eco model.[1] Field data were collected by Nebraska Forest Service summer intern/inventory crews. In the field, 1/6-acre plots were selected based on a random sample with an average density of approximately one plot for every 2,349 acres. The randomly selected plots were categorized to the following land uses: residential and multi-family (89 plots, 44.5 percent of area); commercial/institutional/transport (48 plots, 24.0 percent); "other" (34 plots, 17.0 percent); and agriculture (29 plots, 14.5 percent; Fig. 12).

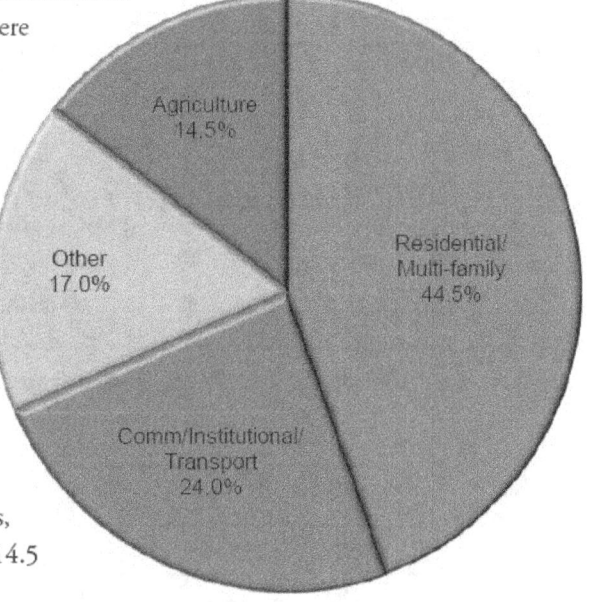

Figure 12.—Land-use distribution, Nebraska, 2008, for inventoried plots.

Tree Characteristics of the Urban Forest

Nebraska has an estimated 13,317,000 urban trees (standard error [SE] of 2,124,000). Urban tree cover is estimated to be 15.0 percent.[13] The five most common species[b] in the urban forest were hackberry (14.9 percent), mulberry (12.6 percent), Siberian elm (11.4 percent), juniper (10.7 percent), and elm (8.6 percent). The 10 most common species account for 77.3 percent of all trees; their relative abundance is illustrated below in Figure 13. Twenty-seven different tree species were sampled in Nebraska; these species and their relative abundance and distribution by land use are presented in Appendix III.

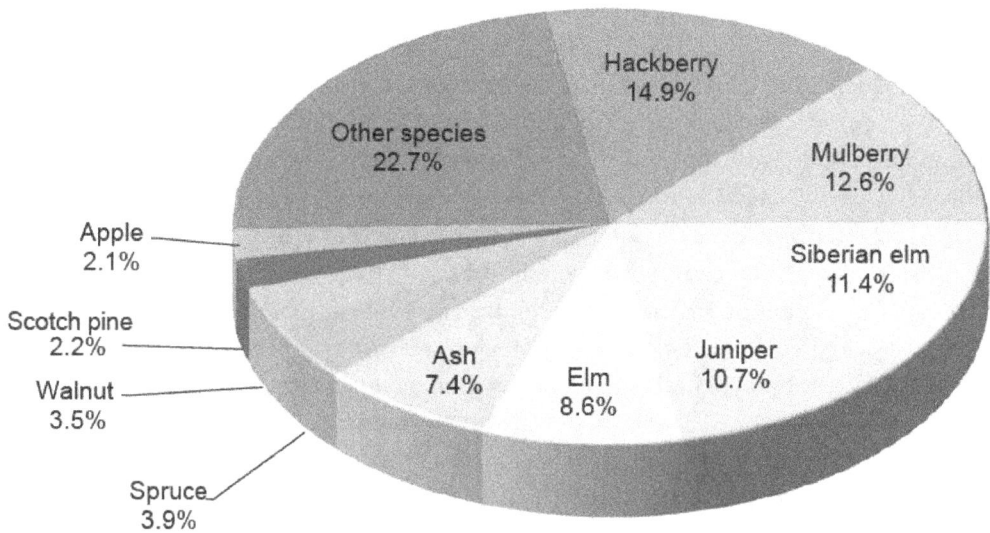

Figure 13.—Urban tree species composition, Nebraska, 2008.

The highest density of trees occurs in "other" land uses (67.2 trees per acre), followed by commercial/institutional/transport (26.9 trees per acre) and residential and multi-family land (22.0 trees per acre; Fig. 14). The overall urban tree density in Nebraska is 28.3 trees per acre, which is relatively low compared to other states' tree densities that range between 3.8 and 182.3 trees per acre (Appendix VI). Trees with diameters less than 6 inches account for 61.5 percent of the population (Figs. 15, 16). Land uses that contain the most leaf area are residential and multi-family lands (48.7 percent of total leaf area) and "other" land uses (31.1 percent).

---

[b] During field data collection, trees sampled in the inventoried plots were classified by genus, though some trees were indentified to the species level. In the event that a tree was identified to the species level (e.g., Siberian elm) and other trees of the same genus were sampled, the genera classification (e.g., elm) includes all sampled trees of the genus that could not be classified to a specific species level. Trees designated as "hardwood" or "softwood" include the sampled trees that could not be identified as a more specific species or genera classification. Since hardwood and softwood are species groups that comprise multiple species and genera, they are not included in the analysis of the most common species. In this report, tree species, genera, or species groups are hereafter referred to as tree species.

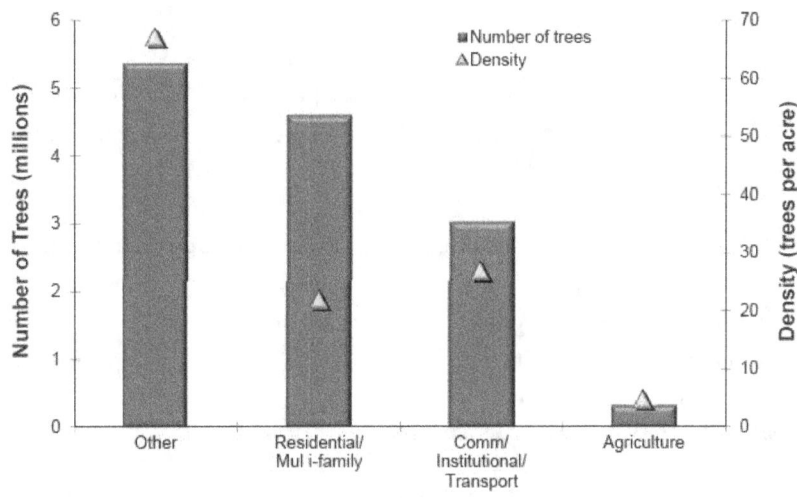

Figure 14.—Number of urban trees and tree density by land use, Nebraska, 2008.

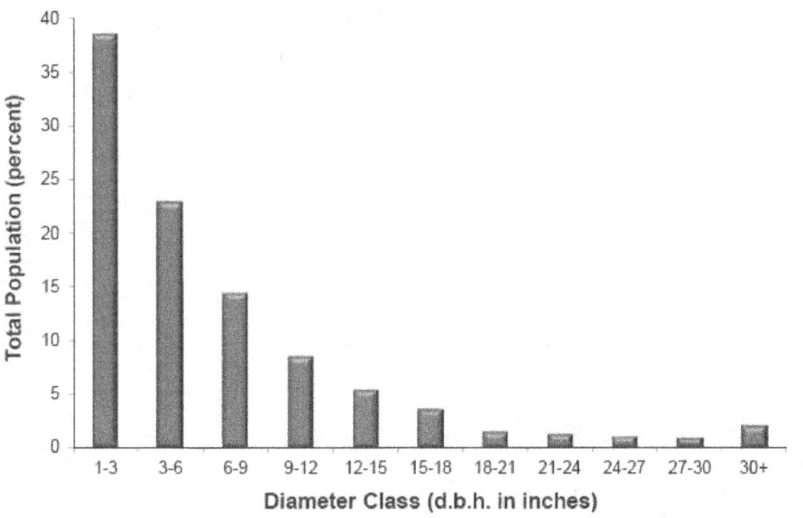

Figure 15.—Percent of total population by diameter class, Nebraska, 2008.

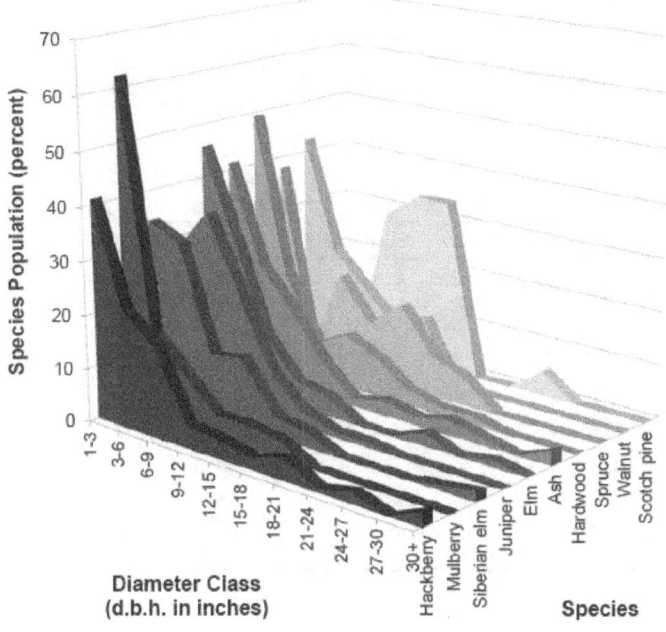

Figure 16.—Percent of species population by diameter class for 10 most common tree species, Nebraska, 2008.

Urban Forest Leaf Area

Many tree benefits are linked to the healthy leaf surface area of the plant, i.e. the greater the leaf area, the greater the benefit. In Nebraska, species with the greatest leaf area are hackberry, Siberian elm, and elm (Fig. 17).

Tree species with relatively large individuals contributing leaf area to the population (species with percent of leaf area much greater than percent of total population) are silver maple, eastern cottonwood, and white oak. Tree species with smaller individuals in the population are boxelder, mulberry, and apple (species with percent of leaf area much less than percentage of total population). The species must also have constituted at least 1 percent of the total population to be considered as relatively large or small trees in the population.

Importance values (IV) are calculated using a formula that takes into account the relative leaf area and relative abundance. High importance values do not mean that these trees should necessarily be used in the future, rather these species currently dominate the urban forest structure. The species in the urban forest with the greatest IVs are hackberry, Siberian elm, and mulberry (Table 7).

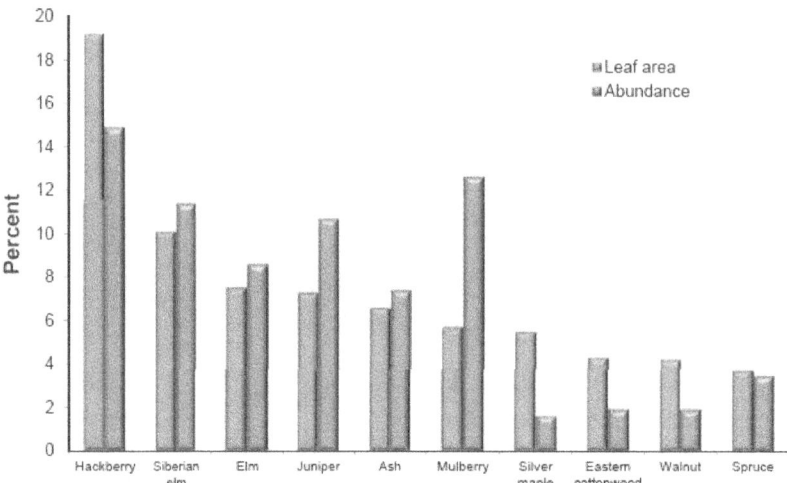

Figure 17.—Percent of total population (abundance) and leaf area for 10 most common tree species, Nebraska, 2008.

Table 7.—Percent of total population, percent of total leaf area, and importance values of species with the greatest importance values, Nebraska, 2008

Common Name	%Pop[a]	%LA[b]	IV[c]
Hackberry	14.9	19.2	34.1
Siberian elm	11.4	10.1	21.5
Mulberry	12.6	5.7	18.3
Juniper	10.7	7.3	18.0
Elm	8.6	7.5	16.1
Ash	7.4	6.6	14.0
Walnut	3.5	4.2	7.7
Spruce	3.9	3.7	7.6
Silver maple	1.6	5.5	7.1
Eastern cottonwood	1.9	4.3	6.2

[a]Percent of total tree population
[b]Percent of total leaf area
[c]IV = %Pop + %LA

Air Pollution Removal by Urban Trees

Poor air quality is a common problem in many urban areas and can lead to human health problems, damage to landscape materials and ecosystem processes, and reduced visibility. The urban forest can help improve air quality by reducing air temperature, directly removing pollutants from the air, and reducing energy consumption in buildings, which consequently reduces air pollutant emissions from power plants. Trees also emit volatile organic compounds that can contribute to ozone formation. However, integrative studies have revealed that an increase in tree cover leads to reduced ozone formation.[17]

Pollution removal by trees in Nebraska was estimated using the i-Tree Eco model in conjunction with field data and hourly pollution and weather data for the year 2000. Pollution removal was greatest for particulate matter less than 10 microns (PM_{10}), followed by ozone (O_3), nitrogen dioxide (NO_2), sulfur dioxide (SO_2), and carbon monoxide (CO) (Fig. 18). It is estimated that trees remove 6,714 tons of air pollution (CO, NO_2, O_3, PM_{10}, SO_2) per year with an associated value of $46.8 million (based on estimated 2007 national median externality costs associated with pollutants[18]). General urban forestry management recommendations to improve air quality are given in Appendix IV.

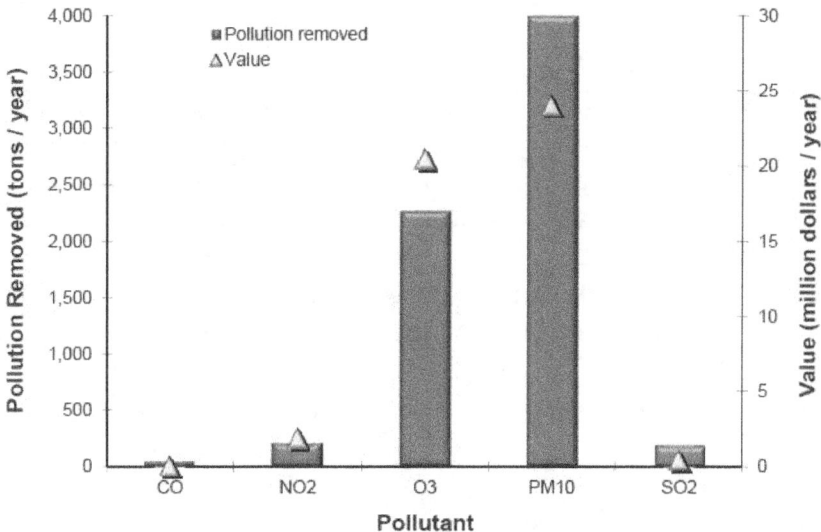

Figure 18.—Annual air pollution removal and value by urban trees, Nebraska, 2008.

Carbon Storage and Sequestration

Climate change is an issue of global concern to many. Urban trees can help mitigate climate change by sequestering atmospheric carbon (from carbon dioxide) in tissue and by reducing energy use in buildings, thus reducing carbon dioxide emissions from fossil-fuel based power plants.[19]

Trees reduce the amount of carbon in the atmosphere by sequestering carbon in new tissue growth. The amount of carbon annually sequestered is increased with healthier and larger diameter trees. Gross sequestration by urban trees in Nebraska is about 84,500 tons of carbon per year (309,900 tons per year of carbon dioxide) with an associated value of $1.7

million per year. Net carbon sequestration in Nebraska is estimated at about 71,300 tons per year (261,500 tons per year of carbon dioxide) based on estimated carbon loss due to tree mortality and decomposition.

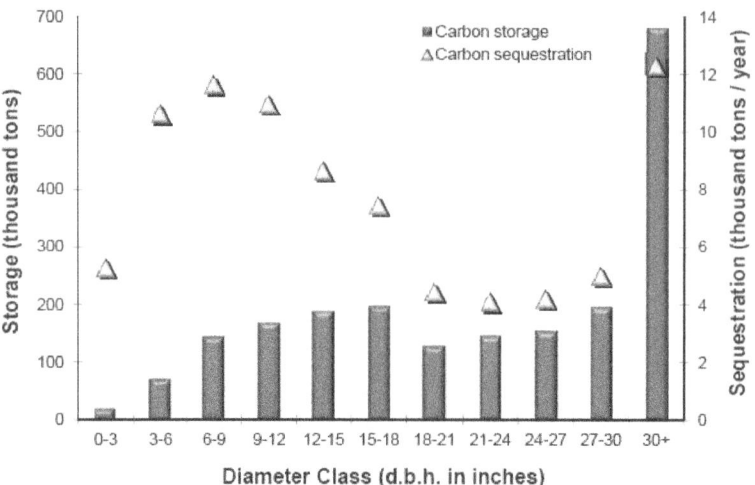

Figure 19.—Total carbon storage and sequestration by diameter class, Nebraska, 2008.

Carbon storage by trees is another way trees can influence global climate change. As trees grow, they store more carbon by holding it in their accumulated tissue. As trees die and decay, they release much of the stored carbon back into the atmosphere. Thus, carbon storage is an indication of the amount of carbon that can be released if trees are allowed to die and decompose. Maintaining healthy trees will keep the carbon stored in trees, but tree maintenance can contribute to carbon emissions.[20] When trees die, utilizing the wood in long-term wood products or to heat buildings or produce energy will help reduce carbon emissions from wood decomposition or from fossil-fuel based power plants. Trees in Nebraska store an estimated 2.1 million tons of carbon (7.7 million tons of carbon dioxide) ($43.4 million; Fig. 19). Of all the species sampled, hackberry stores the most carbon (approximately 17.3 percent of total carbon stored) and annually sequesters the most carbon (18.3 percent of all sequestered carbon; Fig. 20).

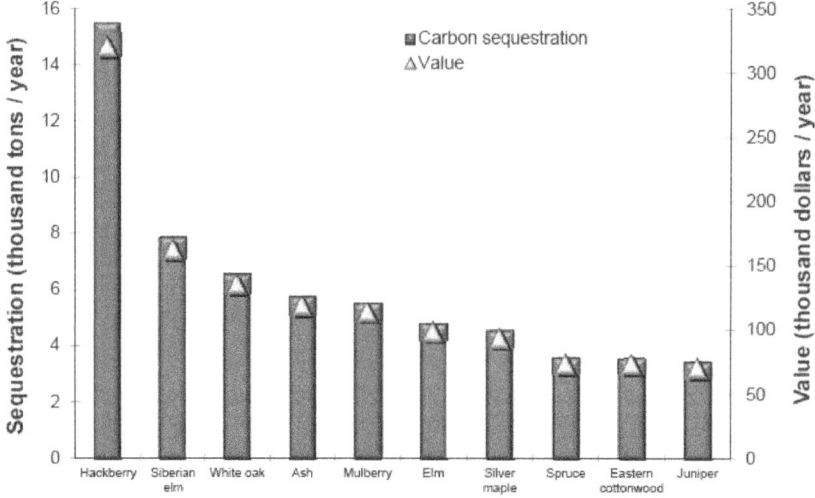

Figure 20.—Annual carbon sequestration and value for urban tree species with the greatest sequestration, Nebraska, 2008.

Trees Affect Energy Use in Buildings

Trees affect energy consumption by shading buildings, providing evaporative cooling, and blocking winter winds. Trees tend to reduce building energy consumption in the summer months and can either increase or decrease building energy use in the winter months, depending on the location of trees around the building. To enhance or sustain evaporative cooling from trees in Nebraska, many trees are or may need to be irrigated. Estimates of tree effects on energy use are based on field measurements of tree distance and direction to space-conditioned residential buildings.[10]

Based on average energy costs in 2007, trees in Nebraska reduce energy costs from residential buildings by an estimated $28.2 million annually (Tables 8, 9). Trees also provide an additional $1.0 million in value per year by reducing the amount of carbon released by fossil-fuel based power plants (a reduction of 48,300 tons of carbon emissions or 177,000 tons of carbon dioxide).

Table 8.—Annual energy savings (MBTU, MWH, and tons) due to trees near residential buildings, Nebraska, 2008

	Heating	Cooling	Total
MBTU[a]	1,813,900	n/a	1,813,900
MWH[b]	12,300	74,200	86,500
Carbon avoided (t)	35,300	13,000	48,300

[a]MBTU – Million British Thermal Units
[b]MWH – Megawatt-hour

Table 9.—Annual monetary savings[c] (dollars) in residential energy expenditures during heating and cooling seasons, Nebraska, 2008

	Heating	Cooling	Total
MBTU[a]	21,697,000	n/a	21,697,000
MWH[b]	927,000	5,579,000	6,506,000
Carbon avoided	730,000	270,000	1,000,000

[a]MBTU – Million British Thermal Units
[b]MWH – Megawatt-hour
[c]Based on 2007 statewide energy costs[13]

Structural and Functional Values

Urban forests have a structural value based on the tree itself, which includes a compensatory value[11] (e.g., the cost of having to replace the tree with a similar tree) and the value of the carbon stored in the tree. The compensatory value of the trees and forests in Nebraska is about $9.8 billion and the carbon storage of Nebraska's trees is estimated at $43.4 million (Fig. 21). The structural value of an urban forest tends to increase with an increase in the number and size of healthy trees.

Urban forests also have functional values (either positive or negative) based on the functions the tree performs. Functional values also tend to increase with increased number and size of healthy trees and are usually on the order of several million dollars per year. There are many other functional values of the urban forest, though they are not quantified here (e.g., reduction in air temperatures and ultraviolet radiation, improvements in water quality,

aesthetics, wildlife habitat, etc.). Through proper management, urban forest values can be increased. However, the values and benefits can also decrease as the amount of healthy tree cover declines.

Urban trees in Nebraska have the following structural values:

- Compensatory value = $9.8 billion
- Carbon storage = $43.4 million

Urban trees in Nebraska have the following annual functional values:

- Carbon sequestration = $1.7 million
- Pollution removal = $46.8 million
- Reduced energy costs = $28.2 million

More detailed information on the urban trees and forests in Nebraska can be found at http://nrs.fs.fed.us/data/urban. Additionally, information on other urban forest values and tree statistics by diameter class can be found in Appendix III.

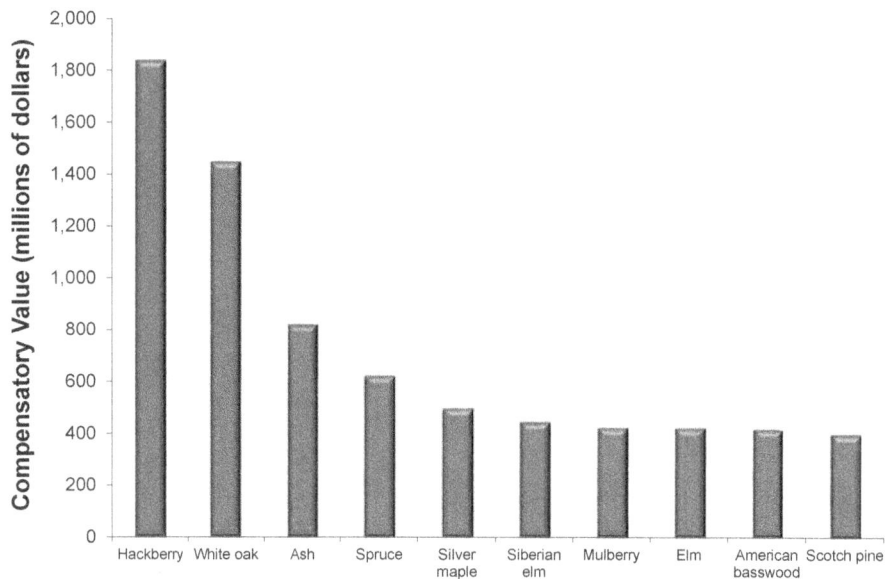

Figure 21.—Tree species with the greatest compensatory value, Nebraska, 2008. Total compensatory value for all trees is $9.8 billion.

Potential Insect and Disease Impacts

Various insects and diseases can infest urban forests, potentially killing trees and reducing the health, value, and sustainability of the urban forest. Various pests have different tree hosts, so the potential damage or risk of each pest will differ. Four exotic pests/diseases were analyzed for their potential impact: Asian longhorned beetle, gypsy moth, emerald ash borer, and Dutch elm disease (Fig. 22). Lists of hosts for these pests/diseases can be found at http://nrs. fs.fed.us/tools/ufore/.

The Asian longhorned beetle (ALB)[21] is an insect that bores into and kills a wide range of hardwood species. This beetle was discovered in 1996 in Brooklyn, NY, and has subsequently spread to Long Island, Queens, and Manhattan. In 1998, the beetle was discovered in the suburbs of Chicago, IL. Beetles have also been found in Jersey City, NJ (2002), Toronto/Vaughan, Ontario (2003), and Middlesex/Union counties, NJ (2004). In 2007, the beetle was found on Staten and Prall's Island, NY. Most recently, beetles were detected in Worcester, MA (2008). This beetle represents a potential loss to Nebraska of $3.4 billion in compensatory value (39.1 percent of live tree population).

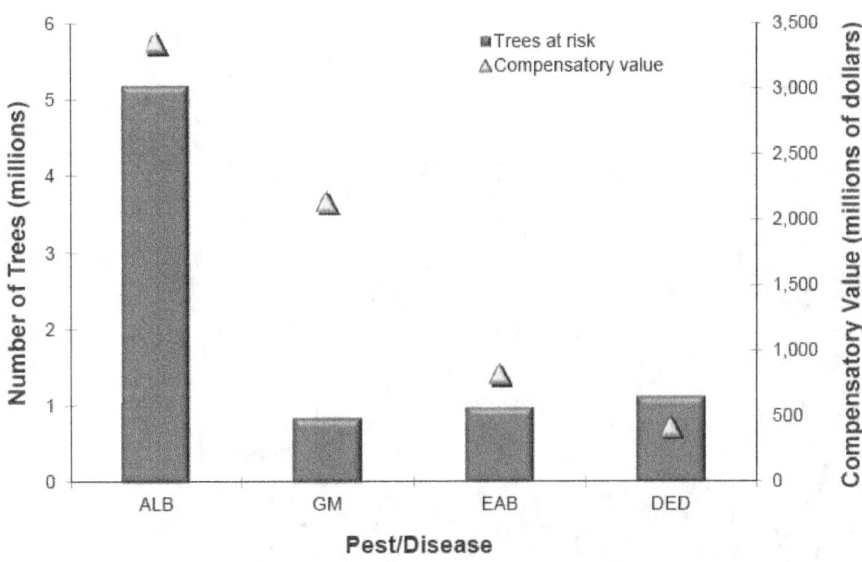

Figure 22.—Number of trees at risk and potential compensatory value of pest/disease effects, Nebraska, 2008.

Gypsy moth (GM)[22] is a defoliator that feeds on many species causing widespread defoliation and tree death if outbreak conditions last several years. This pest could potentially result in damage to or a loss of $2.1 billion in compensatory value of Nebraska's urban trees (6.3 percent of live tree population).

Since being discovered in Detroit in 2002, emerald ash borer (EAB)[23] has killed millions of ash trees in Illinois, Indiana, Iowa, Kentucky, Maryland, Michigan, Minnesota, Missouri, New York, Ohio, Ontario, Pennsylvania, Quebec, Tennessee, Virginia, West Virginia, and Wisconsin. EAB has the potential to affect 7.4 percent of Nebraska's urban tree population ($824 million in compensatory value).

American elm, one of the most important street trees in the 20th century, has been devastated by the Dutch elm disease (DED). Since first reported in the 1930s, it has killed more than 50 percent of the native elm population in the United States.[24] Although some elm species have shown varying degrees of resistance, Nebraska possibly could lose 8.5 percent of its trees to this disease ($424 million in compensatory value).

More information on trees in Nebraska can be found at: http://nrs.fs.fed.us/data/urban.

Gerri Makay, North Dakota Forest Service

26

Introduction

Urban and community forests are highly valued in the Great Plains. An urban or community forest (hereafter referred to as urban forest) refers to the collection of trees, shrubs, and related vegetation growing in cities and towns. These areas include city parks, streetscapes, and trees on public, private, and commercial lands. A large and diverse number of tree species are found in urban and community areas, with the typical North Dakota urban forest dominated by ash, spruce, boxelder, eastern cottonwood, and elm species.

Based on 2000 U.S. Census data, North Dakota has a population of 642,000 people, of which 76.5 percent reside within urban or community areas (areas delimited by census defined incorporated or designated places).[15] The trees and forests in all of these municipalities provide a range of valuable environmental, social, and economic benefits. For every dollar that is invested in the urban forest resource there is typically a positive net annual benefit over the lifespan of a publically owned municipal tree.[16] Many of the urban and community areas in North Dakota rely on state programs, funding, and forestry professionals to maintain healthy urban forest resources. This report provides a platform to further develop urban forest management programs. For more information on the forestry programs and services provided by the state of North Dakota, please refer to Appendix I.

To help assess North Dakota's urban forest, data from 299 field plots located throughout the State were analyzed using the Forest Service's i-Tree Eco model.[1] Field data were collected by North Dakota Forestry staff. In the field, 1/6-acre plots were selected based on a random sample with an average density of approximately one plot for every 869 acres. The randomly selected plots were categorized to the following land uses: agriculture (90 plots, 30.1 percent of area); residential and multi-family (76 plots, 25.4 percent); "other" (55 plots, 18.4 percent); commercial/institutional (52 plots, 17.4 percent); and transportation (26 plots, 8.7 percent; Fig. 23).

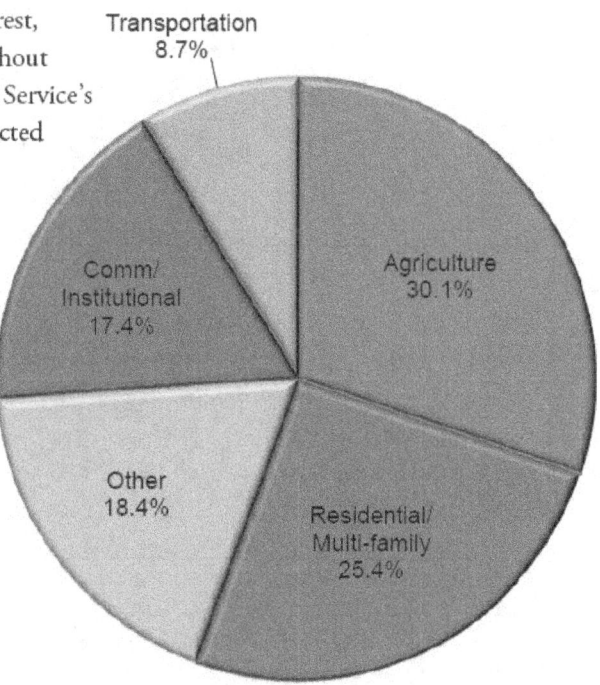

Figure 23.—Land-use distribution, North Dakota, 2008-2009, for inventoried plots.

Tree Characteristics of the Urban Forest

North Dakota has an estimated 975,000 urban trees (standard error [SE] of 171,000). Urban tree cover is estimated to be 2.7 percent.[13] The five most common species[c] in the urban forest were ash (38.5 percent), spruce (13.4 percent), boxelder (8.6 percent), eastern cottonwood (8.0 percent), and elm (6.4 percent). The 10 most common species account for 91.9 percent of all trees; their relative abundance is illustrated in Figure 24. Nineteen different tree species were sampled in North Dakota; these species and their relative abundance and distribution by land use are presented in Appendix IV.

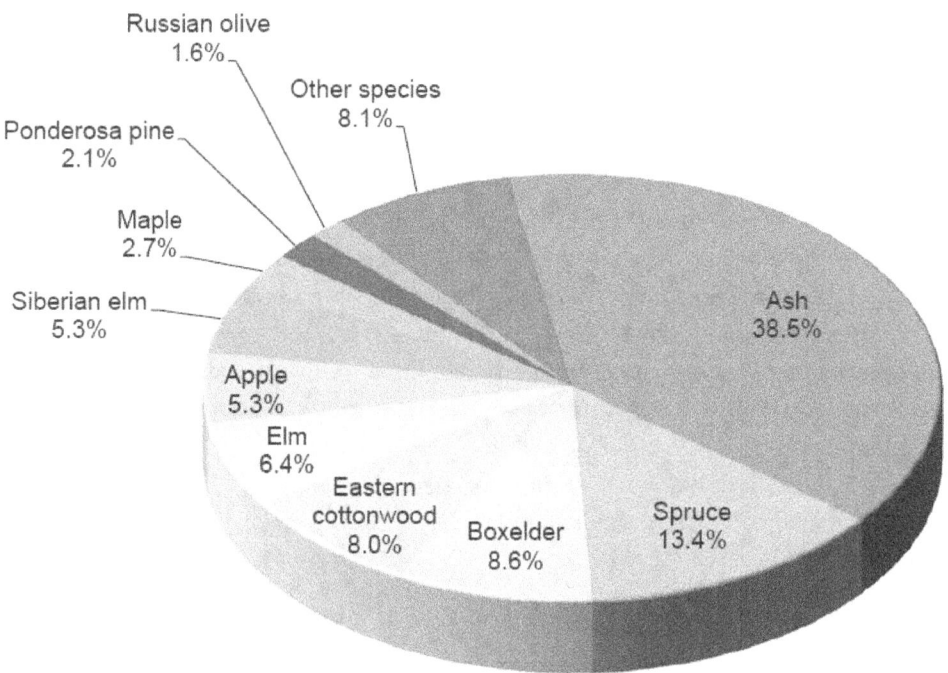

Figure 24.—Urban tree species composition, North Dakota, 2008-2009.

The highest density of trees occurs in residential and multi-family lands (9.7 trees per acre), followed by "other" land uses (2.5 trees per acre), and transportation lands (1.6 trees per acre) (Fig. 25). The overall urban tree density in North Dakota is 3.8 trees per acre, which is the lowest of state tree densities that range between 3.8 and 182.3 trees per acre (Appendix VI). Trees with diameters less than 6 inches account for 35.8 percent of the population (Figs. 26, 27). Land uses that contain the most leaf area are residential and multi-family areas (74.1 percent of total tree leaf area) and "other" land uses (11.4 percent of total tree leaf area).

---

[c] During field data collection, trees sampled in the inventoried plots were classified by genus, though some trees were indentified to the species level. In the event that a tree was identified to the species level (e.g., Siberian elm) and other trees of the same genus were sampled, the genera classification (e.g., elm) includes all sampled trees of the genus that could not be classified to a specific species level. Trees designated as "hardwood" or "softwood" include the sampled trees that could not be identified as a more specific species or genera classification. Since hardwood and softwood are species groups that comprise multiple species and genera, they are not included in the analysis of the most common species. In this report, tree species, genera, or species groups are hereafter referred to as tree species.

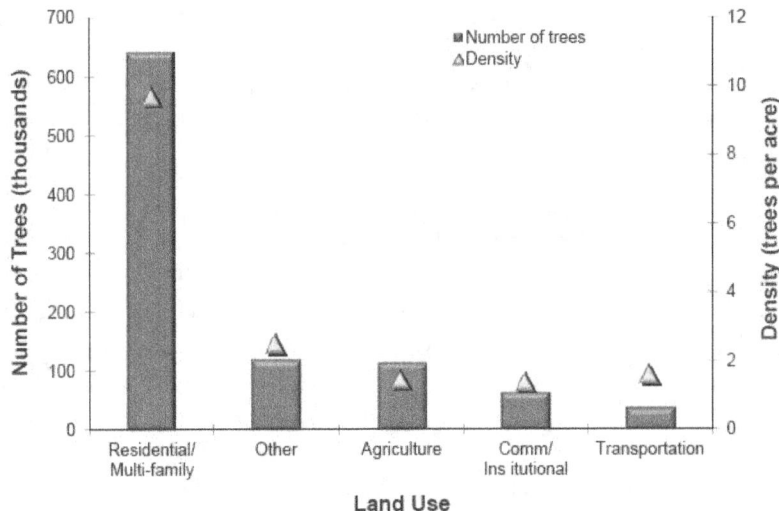

Figure 25.—Number of urban trees and tree density by land use, North Dakota, 2008-2009.

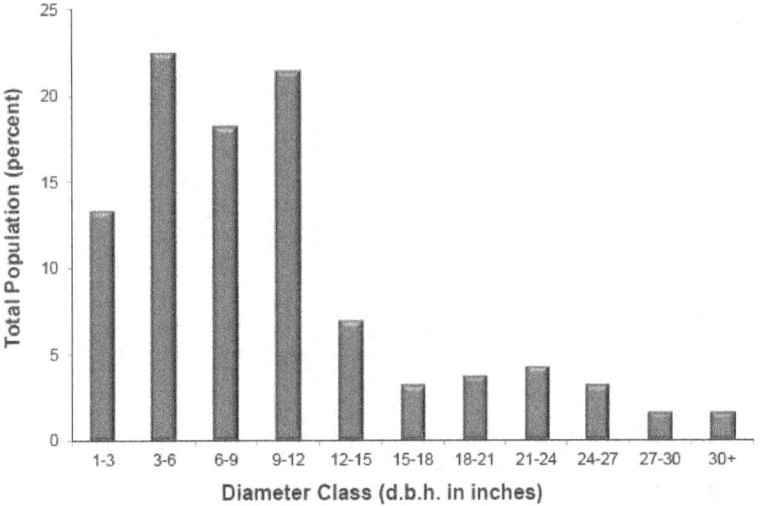

Figure 26.—Percent of total population by diameter class, North Dakota, 2008-2009.

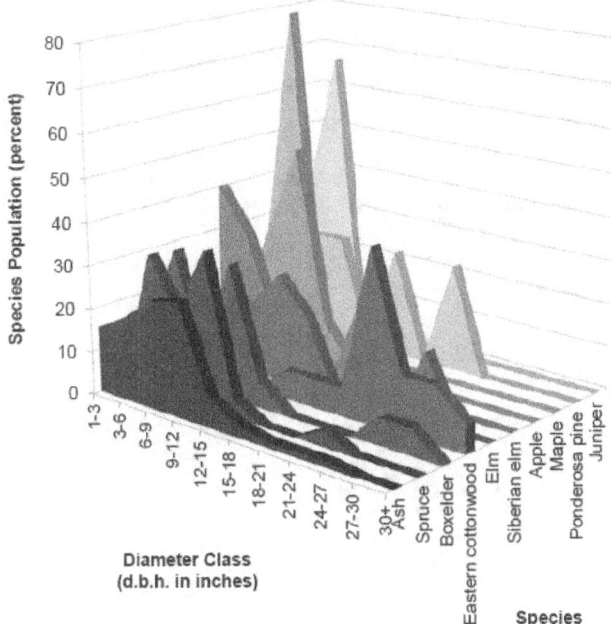

Figure 27.—Percent of species population by diameter class for 10 most common tree species, North Dakota, 2008-2009.

Urban Forest Leaf Area

Many tree benefits are linked to the healthy leaf surface area of the plant, i.e., the greater the leaf area, the greater the benefit. In North Dakota, species with the greatest leaf area are ash, spruce, and eastern cottonwood (Fig. 28).

Tree species with relatively large individuals contributing leaf area to the population (species with percent of leaf area much greater than percentage of total population) are silver maple, eastern cottonwood, and willow. Tree species with smaller individuals in the population are American basswood, white oak, and juniper (species with percent of leaf area much less than percentage of total population). The species must also have constituted at least 1 percent of the total population to be considered as relatively large or small trees in the population.

Importance values (IV) are calculated using a formula that takes into account the relative leaf area and relative abundance. High importance values do not mean that these trees should necessarily be used in the future, rather these species currently dominate the urban forest structure. The species in the urban forest with the greatest IVs are ash, spruce, and eastern cottonwood (Table 10).

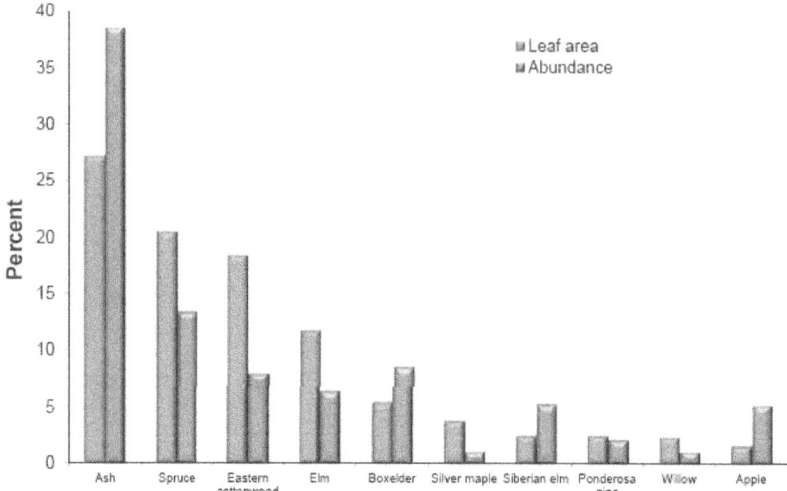

Figure 28.—Percent of total population (abundance) and leaf area for 10 most common tree species, North Dakota, 2008-2009.

Table 10.—Percent of total population, percent of total leaf area, and importance values of species with the greatest importance values, North Dakota, 2008-2009

Common Name	%Pop[a]	%LA[b]	IV[c]
Ash	38.5	27.2	65.7
Spruce	13.4	20.5	33.9
Eastern cottonwood	8.0	18.4	26.4
Elm	6.4	11.8	18.2
Boxelder	8.6	5.4	14.0
Siberian elm	5.3	2.5	7.8
Apple	5.3	1.6	6.9
Silver maple	1.1	3.8	4.9
Ponderosa pine	2.1	2.5	4.6
Maple	2.7	0.8	3.5

[a]Percent of population
[b]Percent of leaf area
[c]IV = %Pop + %LA

Air Pollution Removal by Urban Trees

Poor air quality is a common problem in many urban areas and can lead to human health problems, damage to landscape materials and ecosystem processes, and reduced visibility. The urban forest can help improve air quality by reducing air temperature, directly removing pollutants from the air, and reducing energy consumption in buildings, which consequently reduces air pollutant emissions from power plants. Trees also emit volatile organic compounds that can contribute to ozone formation. However, integrative studies have revealed that an increase in tree cover leads to reduced ozone formation.[17]

Pollution removal by trees in North Dakota was estimated using the i-Tree Eco model in conjunction with field data and hourly pollution and weather data for the year 2000. Pollution removal was greatest for ozone (O_3), followed by particulate matter less than 10 microns (PM_{10}), sulfur dioxide (SO_2), carbon monoxide (CO), and nitrogen dioxide (NO_2) (Fig. 29). It is estimated that trees remove 151 tons of air pollution (CO, NO_2, O_3, PM_{10}, SO_2) per year with an associated value of $1.1 million (based on estimated 2007 national median externality costs associated with pollutants[18]). General urban forestry management recommendations to improve air quality are given in Appendix IV.

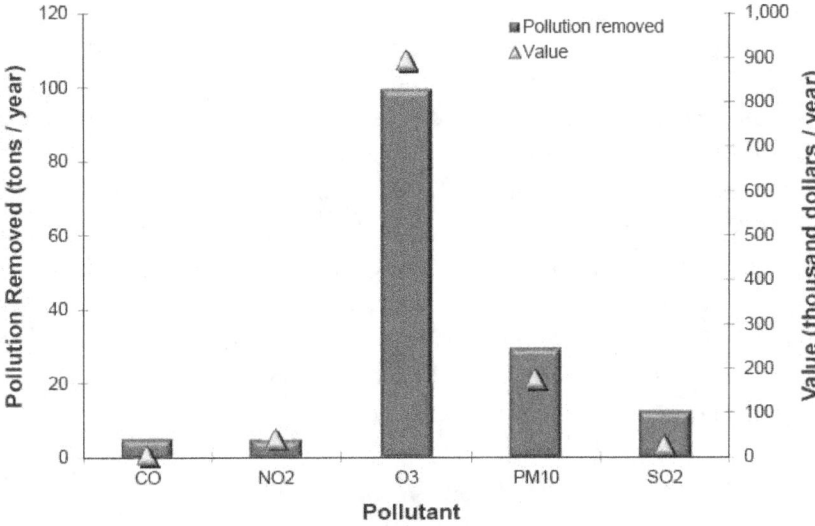

Figure 29.—Annual air pollution removal and value by urban trees, North Dakota, 2008-2009.

Carbon Storage and Sequestration

Climate change is an issue of global concern to many. Urban trees can help mitigate climate change by sequestering atmospheric carbon (from carbon dioxide) in tissue and by reducing energy use in buildings, thus reducing carbon dioxide emissions from fossil-fuel based power plants.[19]

Trees reduce the amount of carbon in the atmosphere by sequestering carbon in new tissue growth. The amount of carbon annually sequestered is increased with healthier and larger diameter trees. Gross sequestration by urban trees in North Dakota is about 8,800 tons of carbon per year (32,300 tons per year of carbon dioxide) with an associated value of

$182,000 per year (Fig. 30). Net carbon sequestration in North Dakota is estimated at about 4,200 tons per year (15,300 tons per year of carbon dioxide) based on estimated carbon loss due to tree mortality and decomposition.

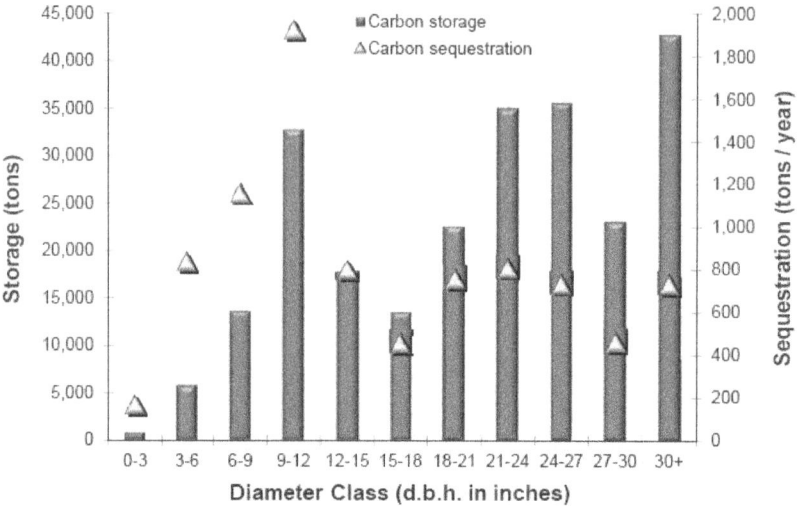

Figure 30.—Total carbon storage and sequestration by diameter class, North Dakota, 2008-2009.

Carbon storage by trees is another way trees can influence global climate change. As trees grow, they store more carbon by holding it in their accumulated tissue. As trees die and decay, they release much of the stored carbon back into the atmosphere. Thus, carbon storage is an indication of the amount of carbon that can be released if trees are allowed to die and decompose. Maintaining healthy trees will keep the carbon stored in trees, but tree maintenance can contribute to carbon emissions.[20] When trees die, utilizing the wood in long-term wood products or to heat buildings or produce energy will help reduce carbon emissions from wood decomposition or from fossil-fuel based power plants. Trees in North Dakota store an estimated 243,000 tons of carbon (893,000 tons of carbon dioxide) ($5.0 million). Of all the species sampled, eastern cottonwood stores the most carbon (approximately 35.7 percent of total carbon stored) and ash annually sequesters the most carbon (29.2 percent of all sequestered carbon; Fig. 31).

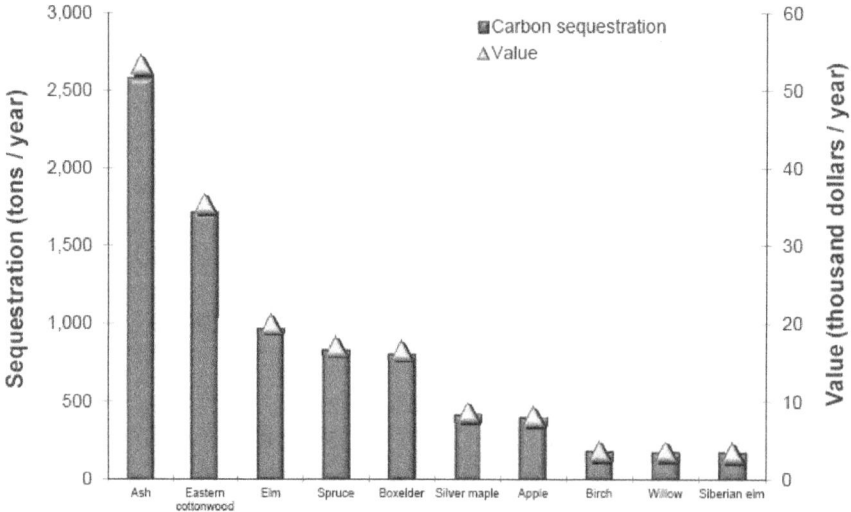

Figure 31.—Annual carbon sequestration and value for urban tree species with the greatest sequestration, North Dakota, 2008-2009.

Trees Affect Energy Use in Buildings

Trees affect energy consumption by shading buildings, providing evaporative cooling, and blocking winter winds. Trees tend to reduce building energy consumption in the summer months and can either increase or decrease building energy use in the winter months, depending on the location of trees around the building. To enhance or sustain evaporative cooling from trees in North Dakota, many trees are or may need to be irrigated. Estimates of tree effects on energy use are based on field measurements of tree distance and direction to space-conditioned residential buildings.[10]

Based on average energy costs in 2007, trees in North Dakota reduce energy costs from residential buildings by an estimated $3.3 million annually (Tables 11, 12). Trees also provide an additional $157,000 in value per year by the reducing amount of carbon released by fossil-fuel based power plants (a reduction of 7,600 tons of carbon emissions or 27,900 tons of carbon dioxide).

Table 11.—Annual energy savings (MBTU, MWH, and tons) due to trees near residential buildings, North Dakota, 2008-2009

	Heating	Cooling	Total
MBTU[a]	211,000	n/a	211,000
MWH[b]	1,700	11,900	13,600
Carbon avoided (t)	3,900	3,700	7,600

[a]MBTU – Million British Thermal Units
[b]MWH – Megawatt-hour

Table 12.—Annual monetary savings[c] (dollars) in residential energy expenditures during heating and cooling seasons, North Dakota, 2008-2009

	Heating	Cooling	Total
MBTU[a]	2,305,000	n/a	2,305,000
MWH[b]	122,000	863,000	985,000
Carbon avoided	80,000	77,000	157,000

[a]MBTU – Million British Thermal Units
[b]MWH – Megawatt-hour
[c]Based on 2007 statewide energy costs[13]

Structural and Functional Values

Urban forests have a structural value based on the tree itself, which includes a compensatory value[11] (e.g., the cost of having to replace the tree with a similar tree) and the value of the carbon stored in the tree. The compensatory value of the trees and forests in North Dakota is about $1.3 billion and the carbon storage of North Dakota's trees is estimated at $5.0 million (Fig. 32).The structural value of an urban forest tends to increase with an increase in the number and size of healthy trees.

Urban forests also have functional values (either positive or negative) based on the functions the tree performs. Functional values also tend to increase with increased number and size of healthy trees and are usually on the order of several million dollars per year. There are many other functional values of the urban forest, though they are not quantified here (e.g., reduction in air temperatures and ultraviolet radiation, improvements in water quality,

aesthetics, wildlife habitat, etc.). Through proper management, urban forest values can be increased. However, the values and benefits can also decrease as the amount of healthy tree cover declines.

Urban trees in North Dakota have the following structural values:

- Compensatory value = $1.3 billion
- Carbon storage = $5.0 million

Urban trees in North Dakota have the following annual functional values:

- Carbon sequestration = $182,000
- Pollution removal = $1.1 million
- Reduced energy costs = $3.3 million

More detailed information on the urban trees and forests in North Dakota can be found at http://nrs.fs.fed.us/data/urban. Additionally, information on other urban forest values and tree statistics by diameter class can be found in Appendix IV.

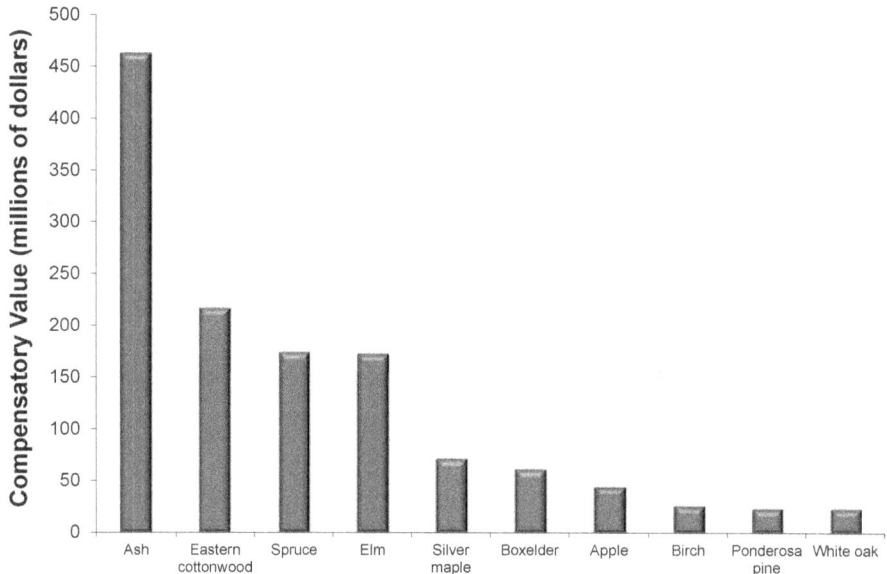

Figure 32.—Tree species with the greatest compensatory value, North Dakota, 2008-2009. Total compensatory value for all trees is $1.3 billion.

Potential Insect and Disease Impacts

Various insects and diseases can infest urban forests, potentially killing trees and reducing the health, value, and sustainability of the urban forest. Various pests have different tree hosts, so the potential damage or risk of each pest will differ. Four exotic pests/diseases were analyzed for their potential impact: Asian longhorned beetle, gypsy moth, emerald ash borer, and Dutch elm disease (Fig. 33). Lists of hosts for these pests/diseases can be found at http://nrs.fs.fed.us/tools/ufore/.

The Asian longhorned beetle (ALB)[21] is an insect that bores into and kills a wide range of hardwood species. This beetle was discovered in 1996 in Brooklyn, NY, and has subsequently spread to Long Island, Queens, and Manhattan. In 1998, the beetle was discovered in the suburbs of Chicago, IL. Beetles have also been found in Jersey City, NJ (2002), Toronto/ Vaughan, Ontario (2003), and Middlesex/Union counties, NJ (2004). In 2007, the beetle was found on Staten and Prall's Island, NY. Most recently, beetles were detected in Worcester, MA (2008). This beetle represents a potential loss to North Dakota of $1.1 billion in compensatory value (80.6 percent of live tree population).

Gypsy moth (GM)[22] is a defoliator that feeds on many species causing widespread defoliation and tree death if outbreak conditions last several years. This pest could potentially result in damage to or a loss of $79 million in compensatory value of North Dakota's urban trees (8.6 percent of live tree population).

Since being discovered in Detroit in 2002, emerald ash borer (EAB)[23] has killed millions of ash trees in Illinois, Indiana, Iowa, Kentucky, Maryland, Michigan, Minnesota, Missouri, New York, Ohio, Ontario, Pennsylvania, Quebec, Tennessee, Virginia, West Virginia, and Wisconsin. EAB has the potential to affect 38.2 percent of North Dakota's urban tree population ($464 million in compensatory value).

American elm, one of the most important street trees in the 20th century, has been devastated by the Dutch elm disease (DED). Since first reported in the 1930s, it has killed more than 50 percent of the native elm population in the United States.[24] Although some elm species have shown varying degrees of resistance, North Dakota possibly could lose 6.5 percent of its trees to this disease ($173 million in compensatory value).

More information on trees in North Dakota can be found at: http://nrs.fs.fed.us/data/urban.

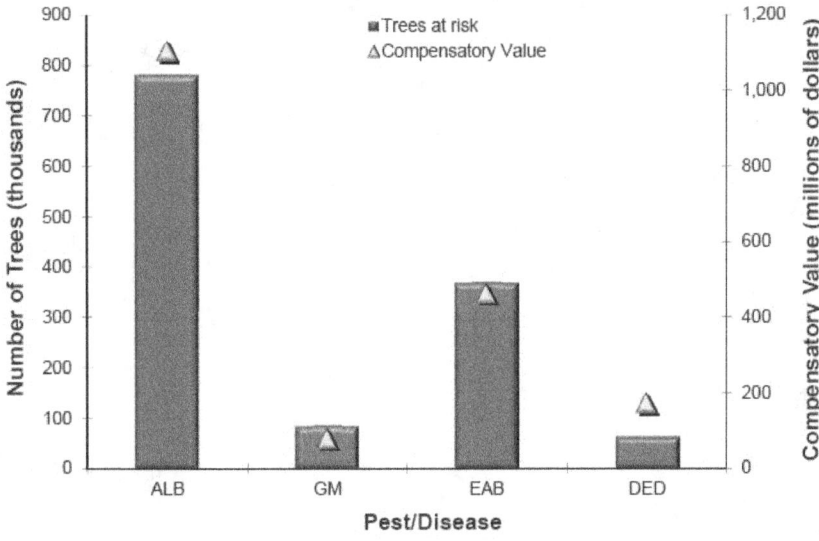

Figure 33.—Number of trees at risk and potential compensatory value of pest/ disease effects, North Dakota, 2008-2009.

Steve Rasmussen, Nebraska Forest Service

Introduction

Urban and community forests are highly valued in the Great Plains. An urban or community forest (hereafter referred to as urban forest) refers to the collection of trees, shrubs, and related vegetation growing in cities and towns. These areas include city parks, streetscapes, and trees on public, private, and commercial lands. A large and diverse number of tree species are found in urban and community areas, with the typical South Dakota urban forest dominated by ponderosa pine, ash, willow, pine, and elm species.

Based on 2000 U.S. Census data, South Dakota has a population of 755,000 people, of which 72.4 percent reside within urban or community areas (areas delimited by census defined incorporated or designated places).[15] The trees and forests in all of these municipalities provide a range of valuable environmental, social, and economic benefits. For every dollar that is invested in the urban forest resource there is typically a positive net annual benefit over the lifespan of a publically owned municipal tree.[16] Many of the urban and community areas in South Dakota rely on state programs, funding, and forestry professionals to maintain healthy urban forest resources. This report provides a platform to further develop urban forest management programs. For more information on the forestry programs and services provided by the state of South Dakota, please refer to Appendix I.

To help assess South Dakota's urban forest, data from 200 field plots located throughout the State were analyzed using the Forest Service's i-Tree Eco model.[1] Field data were collected by summer interns and division service foresters. In the field, 1/6-acre plots were selected based on a random sample with an average density of approximately one plot for every 1,463 acres. The randomly selected plots were categorized to the following land uses: residential-multifamily-farms (57 plots, 28.8 percent of area); "other" (54 plots, 27.3 percent); commercial/institutional/transport (51 plots, 24.7 percent); and agriculture (38 plots, 19.2 percent; Fig. 34).

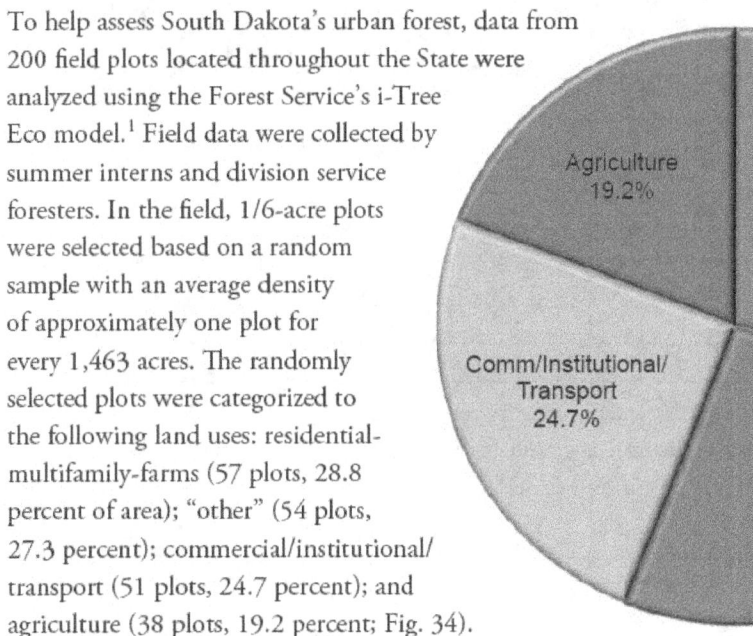

Figure 34.—Land-use distribution, South Dakota, 2008, for inventoried plots.

Tree Characteristics of the Urban Forest

South Dakota has an estimated 5,414,000 urban trees (standard error [SE] of 1,094,000). Urban tree cover is estimated to be 17.0 percent.[13] The five most common species[d] in the urban forest were ponderosa pine (21.3 percent), ash (20.4 percent), willow (9.3 percent), pine (8.3 percent), and elm (5.7 percent). The 10 most common species account for 83.3 percent of all trees; their relative abundance is illustrated in Figure 35. Twenty-six different tree species were sampled in South Dakota; these species and their relative abundance and distribution by land use are presented in Appendix V.

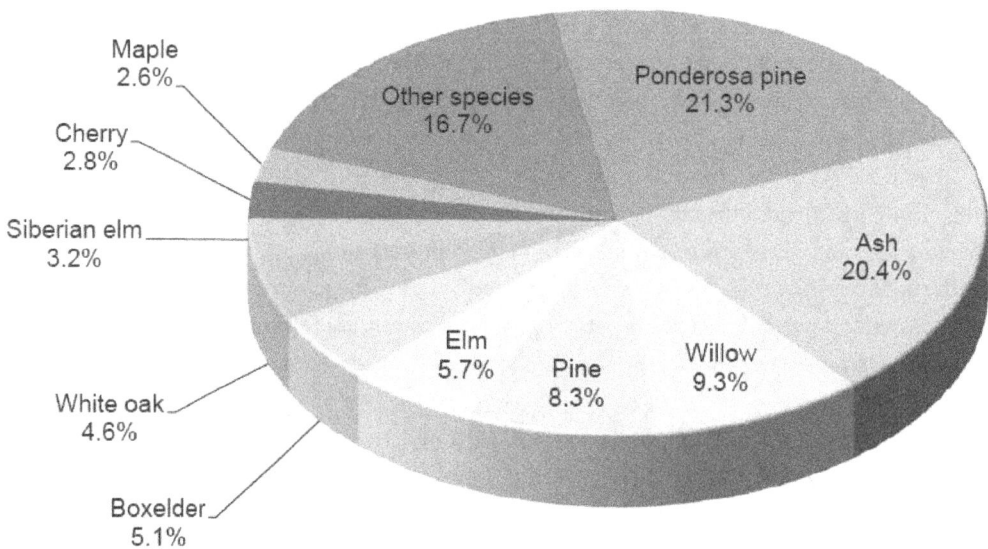

Figure 35.—Urban tree species composition, South Dakota, 2008.

The highest density of trees occurs in "other" (41.6 trees per acre), followed by residential-multifamily-farms (20.4 trees per acre) (Fig. 36). The overall urban tree density in South Dakota is 18.5 trees per acre, which is relatively low compared to other states' tree densities that range between 3.8 and 182.3 trees per acre (Appendix VI). Trees with diameters less than 6 inches account for 49.2 percent of the population (Figs. 37, 38). Land uses that contain the most leaf area are residential-multifamily-farms land use areas (51.3 percent of total tree leaf area) and "other" (38.3 percent).

---

[d] During field data collection, trees sampled in the inventoried plots were classified by genus, though some trees were indentified to the species level. In the event that a tree was identified to the species level (e.g., Siberian elm) and other trees of the same genus were sampled, the genera classification (e.g., elm) includes all sampled trees of the genus that could not be classified to a specific species level. Trees designated as "hardwood" or "softwood" include the sampled trees that could not be identified as a more specific species or genera classification. Since hardwood and softwood are species groups that comprise multiple species and genera, they are not included in the analysis of the most common species. In this report, tree species, genera, or species groups are hereafter referred to as tree species.

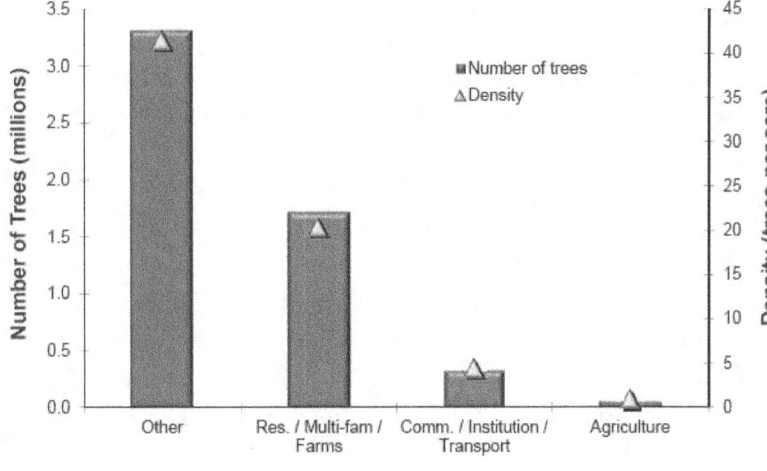

Figure 36.—Number of urban trees and tree density by land use, South Dakota, 2008.

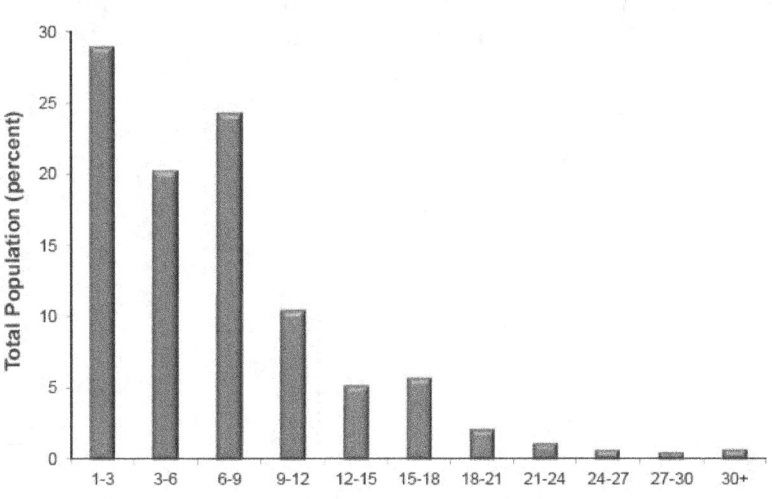

Figure 37.—Percent of total population by diameter class, South Dakota, 2008.

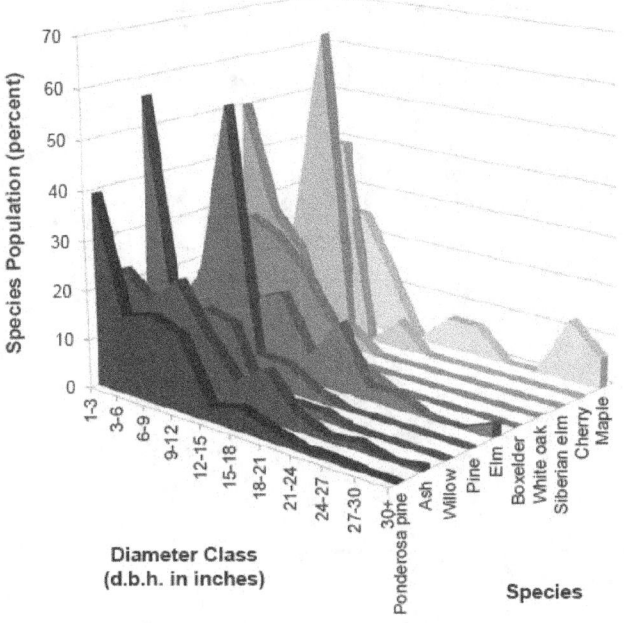

Figure 38.—Percent of species population by diameter class for 10 most common tree species, South Dakota, 2008.

Urban Forest Leaf Area

Many tree benefits are linked to the healthy leaf surface area of the plant, i.e., the greater the leaf area, the greater the benefit. In South Dakota, species with the greatest leaf area are ash, ponderosa pine, and elm (Fig. 39).

Tree species with relatively large individuals contributing leaf area to the population (species with percent of leaf area much greater than percent of total population) are eastern cottonwood, maple, and elm (Fig. 39). Tree species with smaller individuals in the population are pine, white oak, and mulberry (species with percent of leaf area much less than percentage of total population). The species must also have constituted at least 1 percent of the total population to be considered as relatively large or small trees in the population.

Importance values (IV) are calculated using a formula that takes into account the relative leaf area and relative abundance. High importance values do not mean that these trees should necessarily be used in the future, rather these species currently dominate the urban forest structure. The species in the urban forest with the greatest IVs are ash, ponderosa pine, and elm. (Table 13).

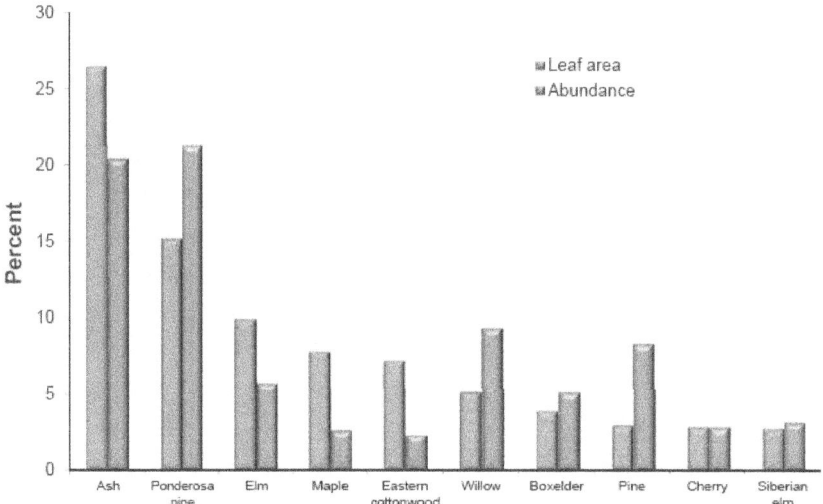

Figure 39.—Percent of total population (abundance) and leaf area for 10 most common tree species, South Dakota, 2008.

Table 13.—Percent of total population, percent of total leaf area, and importance values of species with the greatest importance values, South Dakota, 2008

Common Name	%Pop[a]	%LA[b]	IV[c]
Ash	20.4	26.5	46.9
Ponderosa pine	21.3	15.2	36.5
Elm	5.7	9.9	15.6
Willow	9.3	5.1	14.4
Pine	8.3	2.9	11.2
Maple	2.6	7.8	10.4
Eastern cottonwood	2.3	7.2	9.5
Boxelder	5.1	3.9	9.0
White oak	4.6	1.8	6.4
Siberian elm	3.2	2.7	5.9

[a] Percent of population
[b] Percent of leaf area
[c] IV = %Pop + %LA

Air Pollution Removal by Urban Trees

Poor air quality is a common problem in many urban areas and can lead to human health problems, damage to landscape materials and ecosystem processes, and reduced visibility. The urban forest can help improve air quality by reducing air temperature, directly removing pollutants from the air, and reducing energy consumption in buildings, which consequently reduces air pollutant emissions from power plants. Trees also emit volatile organic compounds that can contribute to ozone formation. However, integrative studies have revealed that an increase in tree cover leads to reduced ozone formation.[17]

Pollution removal by trees in South Dakota was estimated using the i-Tree Eco model in conjunction with field data and hourly pollution and weather data for the year 2000. Pollution removal was greatest for ozone (O_3), followed by particulate matter less than 10 microns (PM_{10}), sulfur dioxide (SO_2), nitrogen dioxide (NO_2), and carbon monoxide (CO) (Fig. 40). It is estimated that trees remove 1,350 tons of air pollution (CO, NO_2, O_3, PM_{10}, SO_2) per year with an associated value of $10.0 million (based on estimated 2007 national median externality costs associated with pollutants[18]). General urban forestry management recommendations to improve air quality are given in Appendix IV.

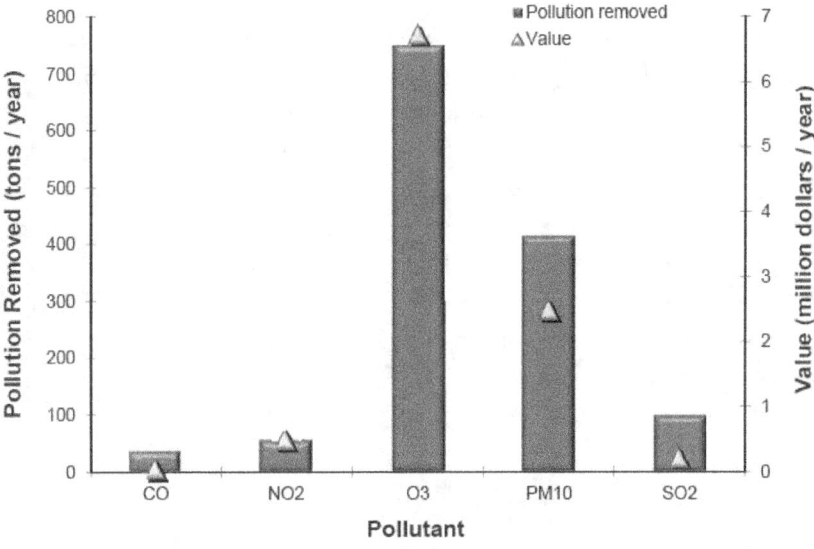

Figure 40.—Annual air pollution removal and value by urban trees, South Dakota, 2008.

Carbon Storage and Sequestration

Climate change is an issue of global concern to many. Urban trees can help mitigate climate change by sequestering atmospheric carbon (from carbon dioxide) in tissue and by reducing energy use in buildings, thus reducing carbon dioxide emissions from fossil-fuel based power plants.[19]

Trees reduce the amount of carbon in the atmosphere by sequestering carbon in new tissue growth. The amount of carbon annually sequestered is increased with healthier and larger diameter trees. Gross sequestration by urban trees in South Dakota is about 28,400 tons of carbon per year (104,200 tons per year of carbon dioxide) with an associated value of

$588,000 per year (Fig. 41). Net carbon sequestration in South Dakota is estimated at about 24,500 tons per year (89,900 tons per year of carbon dioxide) based on estimated carbon loss due to tree mortality and decomposition.

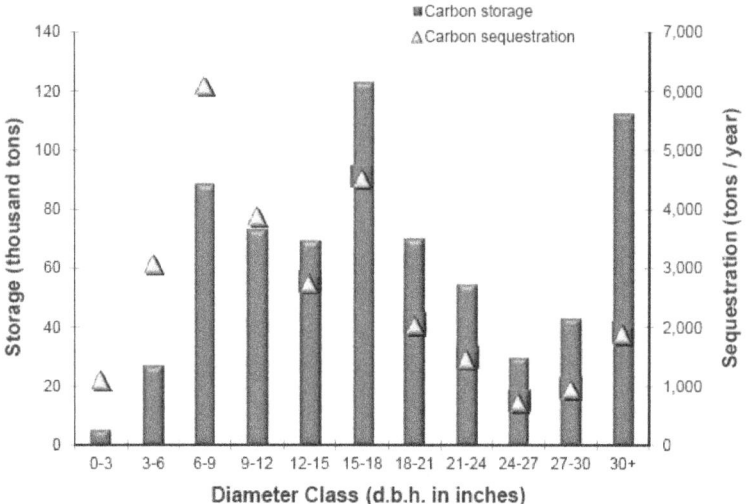

Figure 41.—Total carbon storage and sequestration by diameter class, South Dakota, 2008.

Carbon storage by trees is another way trees can influence global climate change. As trees grow, they store more carbon by holding it in their accumulated tissue. As trees die and decay, they release much of the stored carbon back into the atmosphere. Thus, carbon storage is an indication of the amount of carbon that can be released if trees are allowed to die and decompose. Maintaining healthy trees will keep the carbon stored in trees, but tree maintenance can contribute to carbon emissions.[20] When trees die, utilizing the wood in long-term wood products or to heat buildings or produce energy will help reduce carbon emissions from wood decomposition or from fossil-fuel based power plants. Trees in South Dakota store an estimated 697,000 tons of carbon (2.6 million tons of carbon dioxide) ($14.4 million). Of all the species sampled, ash stores the most carbon (approximately 25.7 percent of total carbon stored) and annually sequesters the most carbon (27.5 percent of all sequestered carbon) (Fig. 42).

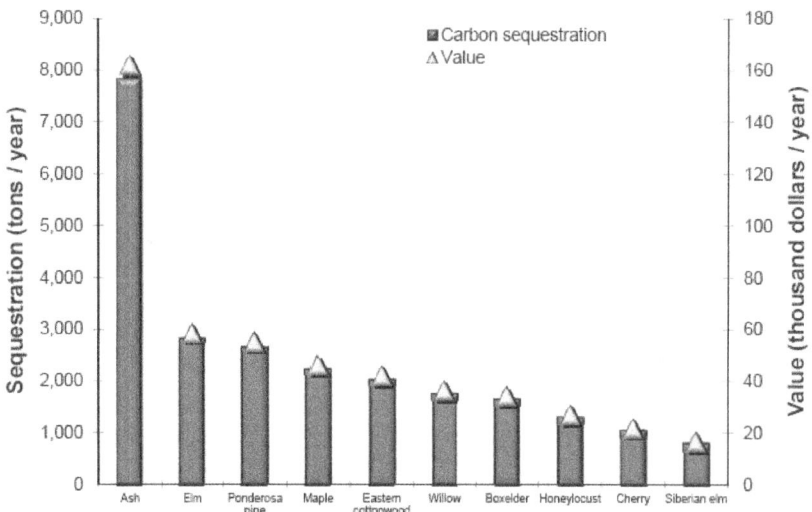

Figure 42.—Annual carbon sequestration and value for urban tree species with the greatest sequestration, South Dakota, 2008.

Trees Affect Energy Use in Buildings

Trees affect energy consumption by shading buildings, providing evaporative cooling, and blocking winter winds. Trees tend to reduce building energy consumption in the summer months and can either increase or decrease building energy use in the winter months, depending on the location of trees around the building. To enhance or sustain evaporative cooling from trees in South Dakota, many trees are or may need to be irrigated. Estimates of tree effects on energy use are based on field measurements of tree distance and direction to space-conditioned residential buildings.[10]

Based on average energy costs in 2007, trees in South Dakota reduce energy costs from residential buildings by an estimated $519,000 annually (Tables 14, 15). Trees also provide an additional $7,300 in value per year by reducing the amount of carbon released by fossil-fuel based power plants (a reduction of 440 tons of carbon emissions or 1,620 tons of carbon dioxide).

Table 14.—Annual energy savings (MBTU, MWH, and tons) due to trees near residential buildings, South Dakota, 2008

	Heating	Cooling	Total
MBTU[a]	-139,000	n/a	-139,000
MWH[b]	-800	28,800	28,000
Carbon avoided (t)	-2,400	2,900	440

[a]MBTU – Million British Thermal Units
[b]MWH – Megawatt-hour

Table 15.—Annual monetary savings[c] (dollars) in residential energy expenditures during heating and cooling seasons, South Dakota, 2008

	Heating	Cooling	Total
MBTU[a]	-1,728,600	n/a	-1,728,600
MWH[b]	-60,600	2,307,800	2,247,200
Carbon avoided	-50,900	58,200	7,300

[a]MBTU – Million British Thermal Units
[b]MWH – Megawatt-hour
[c]Based on 2007 statewide energy costs[13]

Structural and Functional Values

Urban forests have a structural value based on the tree itself, which includes a compensatory value[11] (e.g., the cost of having to replace the tree with a similar tree) and the value of the carbon stored in the tree. The compensatory value of the trees and forests in South Dakota is about $5.1 billion and the carbon storage of South Dakota's trees is estimated at $14.4 million (Figure 43).The structural value of an urban forest tends to increase with an increase in the number and size of healthy trees.

Urban forests also have functional values (either positive or negative) based on the functions the tree performs. Functional values also tend to increase with increased number and size of healthy trees and are usually on the order of several million dollars per year. There are many other functional values of the urban forest, though they are not quantified here (e.g., reduction in air temperatures and ultraviolet radiation, improvements in water quality,

aesthetics, wildlife habitat, etc.). Through proper management, urban forest values can be increased. However, the values and benefits can also decrease as the amount of healthy tree cover declines.

Urban trees in South Dakota have the following structural values:

- Compensatory value = $5.1 billion
- Carbon storage = $14.4 million

Urban trees in South Dakota have the following annual functional values:

- Carbon sequestration = $588,000
- Pollution removal = $10.0 million
- Reduced energy costs = $519,000

More detailed information on the urban trees and forests in South Dakota can be found at http://nrs.fs.fed.us/data/urban. Additionally, information on other urban forest values and tree statistics by diameter class can be found in Appendix V.

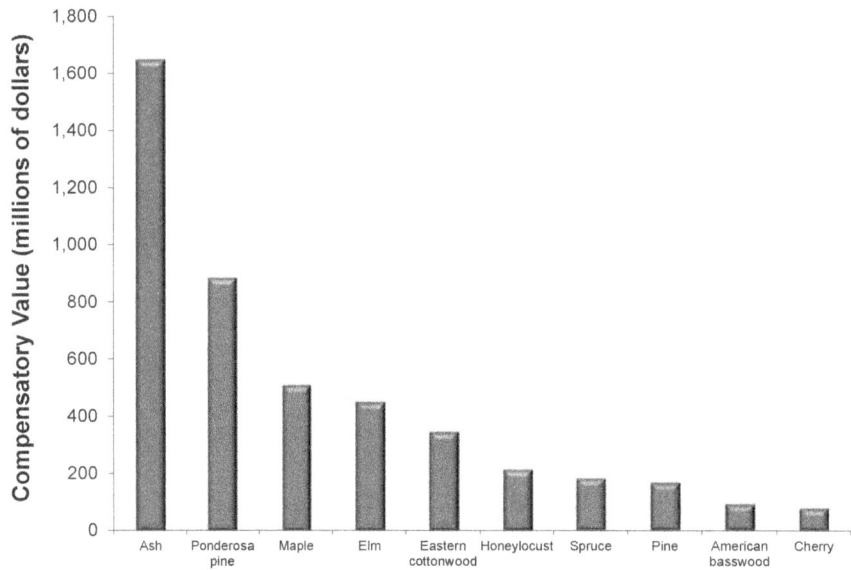

Figure 43.—Tree species with the greatest compensatory value, South Dakota, 2008-2009. Total compensatory value for all trees is $5.1 billion.

Potential Insect and Disease Impacts

Various insects and diseases can infest urban forests, potentially killing trees and reducing the health, value, and sustainability of the urban forest. Various pests have different tree hosts, so the potential damage or risk of each pest will differ. Four exotic pests/diseases were analyzed for their potential impact: Asian longhorned beetle, gypsy moth, emerald ash borer, and Dutch elm disease (Fig. 44). Lists of hosts for these pests/diseases can be found at http://nrs. fs.fed.us/tools/ufore/.

The Asian longhorned beetle (ALB)[21] is an insect that bores into and kills a wide range of hardwood species. This beetle was discovered in 1996 in Brooklyn, NY, and has subsequently spread to Long Island, Queens, and Manhattan. In 1998, the beetle was discovered in the suburbs of Chicago, IL. Beetles have also been found in Jersey City, NJ (2002), Toronto/ Vaughan, Ontario (2003), and Middlesex/Union counties, NJ (2004). In 2007, the beetle was found on Staten and Prall's Island, NY. Most recently, beetles were detected in Worcester, MA (2008). This beetle represents a potential loss to South Dakota of $3.4 billion in compensatory value (54.4 percent of live tree population).

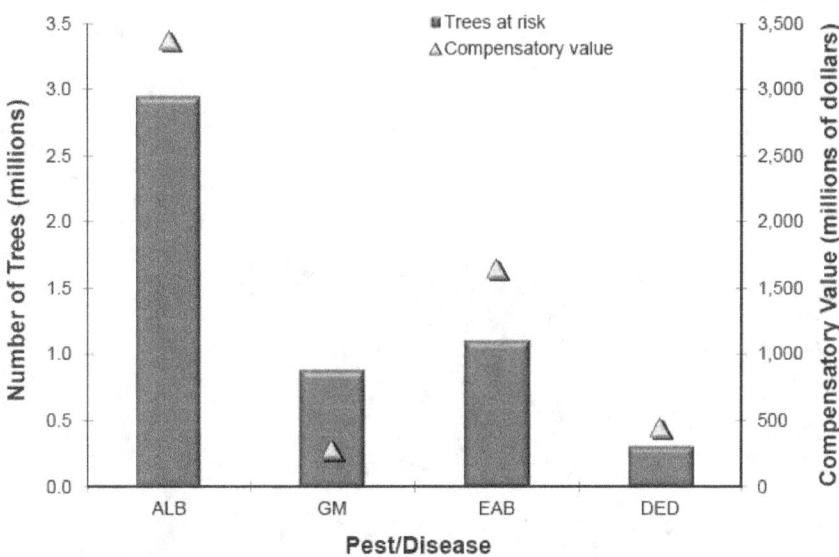

Figure 44.—Number of trees at risk and potential compensatory value of pest/disease effects, South Dakota, 2008.

Gypsy moth (GM)[22] is a defoliator that feeds on many species causing widespread defoliation and tree death if outbreak conditions last several years. This pest could potentially result in damage to or a loss of $285 million in compensatory value of South Dakota's urban trees (16.4 percent of live tree population).

Since being discovered in Detroit in 2002, emerald ash borer (EAB)[23] has killed millions of ash trees in Illinois, Indiana, Iowa, Kentucky, Maryland, Michigan, Minnesota, Missouri, New York, Ohio, Ontario, Pennsylvania, Quebec, Tennessee, Virginia, West Virginia, and Wisconsin. EAB has the potential to affect 20.4 percent of South Dakota's urban tree population ($1.7 billion in compensatory value).

American elm, one of the most important street trees in the 20th century, has been devastated by the Dutch elm disease (DED). Since first reported in the 1930s, it has killed more than 50 percent of the native elm population in the United States.[24] Although some elm species have shown varying degrees of resistance, South Dakota possibly could lose 5.7 percent of its trees to this disease ($451 million in compensatory value).

More information on trees in South Dakota can be found at: http://nrs.fs.fed.us/data/urban.

CONCLUSION

The urban forests of the Great Plains states provide millions of dollars of benefits annually to local residents, but some of these benefits could be lost in the future due to insect or disease infestations or improper planning of management. Data from this report provides the basis for a better understanding of the urban forest resource and estimates of the ecosystem services and values provided by this resource. Managers and citizens can use these data to help develop improved long-term management plans and policies to sustain a healthy urban tree population and ecosystem services for future generations. Improved planning and management to sustain healthy tree populations can lead to improved environmental quality and quality of life for Great Plains residents.

Steve Rasmussen, Nebraska Forest Service

REFERENCES

1 Nowak, D.J.; Crane, D.E. 2000. **The Urban Forest Effects (UFORE) Model: quantifying urban forest structure and functions.** In: Hansen, M.; Burk, T., eds. Integrated tools for natural resources inventories in the 21st century. Proceedings of IUFRO conference. Gen. Tech. Rep. NC-212. St. Paul, MN: U.S. Department of Agriculture, Forest Service, North Central Research Station: 714-720.

   Nowak, D.J.; Hoehn, R.E.; Crane, D.E.; Stevens, J.C.; Walton, J.T.; and Bond, J. 2008. **A ground-based method of assessing urban forest structure and ecosystem services.** Arboriculture and Urban Forestry. 34(6): 347-358

   i-Tree Eco model was formerly named the Urban Forest Effects (UFORE) model.

2 Nowak, D.J.; Greenfield, E.J. 2010. **Urban and community forests of the North Central West region: Iowa, Kansas, Minnesota, Missouri, Nebraska, North Dakota, South Dakota.** Gen. Tech. Rep. NRS-56. Newtown Square, PA: U.S. Department of Agriculture, Forest Service, Northern Research Station. 70 p.

3 i-Tree. **2009 i-Tree Eco manual. Version 4.1.0.** 113 p. http://www.itreetools.org/ resource_learning_center/manuals_workbooks.shtm

4 Nowak, D.J. 1994. **Atmospheric carbon dioxide reduction by Chicago's urban forest.** In: McPherson, E.G.; Nowak, D.J.; Rowntree, R.A., eds. Chicago's urban forest ecosystem: results of the Chicago Urban Forest Climate Project. Gen. Tech. Rep. NE-186. Radnor, PA: U.S. Department of Agriculture, Forest Service, Northeastern Forest Experiment Station: 83-94.

5 Baldocchi, D. 1988. **A multi-layer model for estimating sulfur dioxide deposition to a deciduous oak forest canopy.** Atmospheric Environment. 22: 869-884.

6 Baldocchi, D.D.; Hicks, B.B.; Camara, P. 1987. **A canopy stomatal resistance model for gaseous deposition to vegetated surfaces.** Atmospheric Environment. 21: 91-101.

7 Bidwell, R.G.S.; Fraser, D.E. 1972. **Carbon monoxide uptake and metabolism by leaves.** Canadian Journal of Botany. 50: 1435-1439.

8 Lovett, G.M. 1994. **Atmospheric deposition of nutrients and pollutants in North America: an ecological perspective.** Ecological Applications. 4:629-650.

9 Zinke, P.J. 1967. **Forest interception studies in the United States.** In: Sopper, W.E.; Lull, H.W., eds. Forest hydrology. Oxford, UK: Pergamon Press: 137-161.

10 McPherson, E.G.; Simpson, J.R. 1999. **Carbon dioxide reduction through urban forestry: guidelines for professional and volunteer tree planters.** Gen. Tech. Rep.

PSW-171. Albany, CA: U.S. Department of Agriculture, Forest Service, Pacific Southwest Research Station. 237 p.

11 Nowak, D.J.; Crane, D.E.; Dwyer, J.F. 2002. **Compensatory value of urban trees in the United States**. Journal of Arboriculture. 28(4): 194-199.

12 Nowak, D.J.; Crane, D.E.; Stevens, J.C.; Ibarra, M. 2002. **Brooklyn's urban forest.** Gen. Tech. Rep. NE-290. Newtown Square, PA: U.S. Department of Agriculture, Forest Service, Northeastern Research Station. 107 p.

13 Tree cover is estimated by field plots or photo interpretation of Google imagery. Typically photo interpretation is a better estimate of tree cover because field plot estimates are based on crown width measurements on the plot. Photo interpretation for urban or community land in each state was conducted as part of national cover estimate and was reported in: Nowak, D.J.; Greenfield, E.J. **Tree and impervious cover in the United States.** 2012. Landscape and Urban Planning. 107: 21-30.

Each of the four Great Plain States had a sample size of 100 points for photo-interpretation, but greater than 100 plots in the field data collection.

Due to the larger sample size, field crew estimates of urban tree cover were used for Kansas, North Dakota, and South Dakota. However, in Nebraska, it is believed that the field plot estimates of urban tree cover are too low based on testing against tree density per unit cover and diameter (d.b.h.) distribution. Thus, urban tree cover for Nebraska was based on the photo interpretation estimates of 15.0 percent with a standard error of 3.6 percent.

14 Energy costs are derived from the U.S. Energy Information Administration based on 2007 state average costs for natural gas (http://tonto.eia.doe.gov/dnav/ng/ng_pri_sum_a_EPG0_PRS_DMcf_a.htm); 2007/2008 heating season fuel oil costs (http://tonto.eia.doe.gov/OOG/INFO/HOPU/hopu.asp); 2007 electricity costs (http://www.eia.doe.gov/electricity/page/sales_revenue.xls) and 2005 costs of wood (http://www.eia.doe.gov/emeu/states/sep_sum/html/sum_pr_tot.html).

15 U.S. Census Bureau. 2000. **Urban/Rural and Metropolitan/Nonmetropolitan Population: 2000—State Urban/Rural and Inside/Outside Metropolitan Area** [dataset]. GCT-P1. Washington, DC: U.S. Department of Commerce, Bureau of the Census.

16 McPherson, E.G.; Simpson, J.R.; Peper, P.J.; Gardner, S.L.; Vargas, K.E.; Maco, S.E.; Xiao, Q. 2006. **Midwest community tree guide: benefits, costs, and strategic planting**. Gen. Tech. Rep. PSW-GTR-199. Albany, CA: U.S. Department of Agriculture, Forest Service, Pacific Southwest Research Station. 99 p.

17 Nowak D.J.; Dwyer, J.F. 2000. **Understanding the benefits and costs of urban forest ecosystems.** In: Kuser, John E., ed. Handbook of urban and community forestry in the northeast. New York, NY: Kluwer Academics/Plenum: 11-22.

18 Murray, F.J.; Marsh L.; Bradford, P.A. 1994. **New York state energy plan, vol. II: issue reports.** Albany, NY: New York State Energy Office. These values were updated to 2007 dollars based on the producer price index from U.S Department of Labor, Bureau of Labor Statistics. www.bls.gov/ppi

19 Abdollahi, K.K.; Ning, Z.H.; Appeaning, A., eds. 2000. **Global climate change and the urban forest.** Baton Rouge, LA: GCRCC and Franklin Press. 77 p. Carbon values are estimated at $22.8 USD per tonne based on: Fankhauser, S. 1994. **The social costs of greenhouse gas emissions: an expected value approach**. The Energy Journal. 15(2): 157-184.

20 Nowak, D.J.; Stevens, J.C.; Sisinni, S.M.; Luley, C.J. 2002. **Effects of urban tree management and species selection on atmospheric carbon dioxide.** Journal of Arboriculture. 28(3):113-122.

21 Animal and Plant Health Inspection Service. 2010. **Plant health—Asian longhorned beetle.** Washington, DC: U.S. Department of Agriculture, Animal and Plant Health Inspection Service. http://www.aphis.usda.gov/plant_health/plant_pest_info/asian_lhb/index.shtml

   Natural Resources Canada. 2011. **Trees, insects, and diseases of Canada's forests - Asian longhorned beetle**. https://tidcf.nrcan.gc.ca/insects/factsheet/1000095

22 Northeastern Area State and Private Forestry. 2005. **Gypsy moth digest.** Newtown Square, PA: U.S. Department of Agriculture, Forest Service, Northeastern Area State and Private Forestry. http://www.na.fs.fed.us/fhp/gm/

23 Michigan State University. 2010. **Emerald ash borer**. East Lansing, MI: Michigan State University [and others]. http://www.emeraldashborer.info/

24 Stack, R.W.; McBride, D.K.; Lamey, H.A. 1996. **Dutch elm disease.** PP-324 (revised). Fargo, ND: North Dakota State University, Cooperative Extension Service. http://www.ext.nodak.edu/extpubs/plantsci/trees/pp324w.htm

Explanation of Calculations for Appendix II, III, IV, V and VI

25 Total carbon emissions were based on 2003 U.S. per capita carbon emissions, calculated as total U.S. carbon emissions (Energy Information Administration, 2003, Emissions of Greenhouse Gases in the United States 2003. http://www.eia.doe.gov/ oiaf/1605/1605aold.html) divided by 2003 total U.S. population (www.census.gov). Per capita emissions were multiplied by study population to estimate total city carbon emissions.

26 Average passenger automobile emissions per mile were based on dividing total 2002 pollutant emissions from light-duty gas vehicles (National Emission Trends http:// www.epa.gov/ttn/chief/ trends/index.html) by total miles driven in 2002 by passenger cars (National Transportation Statistics http://www.bts.gov/publications/national_ transportation_statistics/2004/).

Average annual passenger automobile emissions per vehicle were based on dividing total 2002 pollutant emissions from light-duty gas vehicles by total number of passenger cars in 2002 (National Transportation Statistics http://www. bts.gov/publications/national_ transportation_statistics/2004/).

Carbon dioxide emissions from automobiles assumed 6 pounds of carbon per gallon of gasoline with energy costs of refinement and transportation included (Graham, R.L.; Wright, L.L.; Turhollow, A.F. 1992. The potential for short-rotation woody crops to reduce U.S. CO2 emissions. Climatic Change. 22:223-238.)

27 Average household emissions based on average electricity kWh usage, natural gas Btu usage, fuel oil Btu usage, kerosene Btu usage, LPG Btu usage, and wood Btu usage per household from:

Energy Information Administration. 2004. Total energy consumption in U.S. households by type of housing unit, 2001. Washington, DC: U.S. Department of Energy, Energy Information Administration. http://www.eia.gov/emeu/recs/recs2001/ce_pdf/enduse/ ce1-4c_housingunits2001.pdf

CO2, SO2, and NOx power plant emission per KWh from:

U.S. Environmental Protection Agency. U.S. power plant emissions total by year http:// www.epa.gov/cleanenergy/energy-resources/egrid/index.html

CO emission per kWh assumes one-third of 1 percent of C emissions is CO based on:

Energy Information Administration. 1994. Energy use and carbon emissions: non-OECD countries. DOE/EIA-0579(94). Washington, DC: Department of Energy, Energy Information Administration. http://tonto.eia.doe.gov/bookshelf

PM10 emission per kWh from:

Layton, M. 2004. 2005 Electricity environmental performance report: electricity generation and air emissions. Sacramento, CA: California Energy Commission. http://www.energy.ca.gov/2005_energypolicy/documents/2004-11-15_ workshop/2004-11-15_03- A_LAYTON.PDF

CO2, NOx, SO2, PM10, and CO emission per Btu for natural gas, propane and butane (average used to represent LPG), Fuel #4 and #6 (average used to represent fuel oil and kerosene) from:

Abraxas energy consulting. http://www abraxasenergy.com/emissions/

CO2 and fine particle emissions per Btu of wood from:

Houck, J.E.; Tiegs, P.E.; McCrillis, R.C.; Keithley, C.; Crouch, J. 1998. **Air emissions from residential heating: the wood heating option put into environmental perspective**. In: Proceedings of U.S. EPA and Air and Waste Management Association conference: living in a global environment, V.1: 373-384.

CO, NOx and SOx emission per Btu of wood based on total emissions from wood burning (tonnes) from:

Residential Wood Burning Emissions in British Columbia. 2005. http://www.env.gov. bc.ca/air/airquality/pdfs/wood_emissions.pdf.

Emissions per dry tonne of wood converted to emissions per Btu based on average dry weight per cord of wood and average Btu per cord from:

Kuhns, M.; Schmidt, T. 1988. Heating with wood: species characteristics and volumes I. NebGuide G-88-881-A. Lincoln, NE: University of Nebraska, Institute of Agriculture and Natural Resources, Cooperative Extension.

28 Nowak, D.J.; Cumming, A.B.; Twardus, D.; Hoehn, R.E.; Oswalt, C.M.; Brandeis, T.J. 2011. **Urban forests of Tennessee, 2009**. Gen. Tech. Rep. SRS-149. Asheville, NC: U.S. Department of Agriculture, Forest Service, Southern Research Station. 52 p.

29 Cumming, A.B.; Nowak, D.; Twardus, D.; Hoehn, R.; Mielke, M.; Rideout, R. 2007. **National Forest Health Monitoring Program, urban forests of Wisconsin: Pilot Monitoring Project 2002**. NA-FR-05-07. Newtown Square, PA: U.S. Department of Agriculture, Forest Service, Northeastern Area State and Private Forestry. 33 p.

30 Nowak, D.; Cumming, A.B.; Twardus, D.; Hoehn, R.; Mielke, M. 2007. **National Forest Health Monitoring Program, Monitoring Urban Forests in Indiana: Pilot Study 2002, Part 2: Statewide Estimates Using the UFORE Model**. Northeastern Area Report. NA-FR-01-07. Newtown Square, PA: U.S. Department of Agriculture, Forest Service, Northeastern Area State and Private Forestry. 13 p.

APPENDICES

Appendix I. State Urban Forestry Programs

Many of the urban and community areas in Kansas, Nebraska, North Dakota, and South Dakota rely on state programs, funding, and forestry professionals to maintain healthy urban forest resources.

Kansas

Urban and community forestry is the planting and management of trees and green spaces on publicly owned properties, such as parks, greenbelts, natural areas, and rights-of-way (city easements). In Kansas, the state forestry program: Community Forestry, is responsible for a number of programs that benefit the general public in relation to urban and community forestry. The general goal of this program is to create safe, healthy, sustainable and more livable communities by integrating trees and plants into Kansas' cities and towns.

The urban and community foresters of Kansas provide assistance to communities by targeting the following priority areas: technical assistance, education and training, resource development, and public awareness. The Community Forestry Program also administers programs in Kansas such as Tree City USA, Arbor Day Poster Contest, Arborists Training, and the Champion Tree Program.

Nebraska

Nebraska Forest Service's (NFS) Community Forestry & Sustainable Landscape program annually cooperates with more than 140 communities. One of the cornerstones of this program effort is the national Tree City USA program sponsored by the Arbor Day Foundation and administered statewide by the NFS. The NFS also provides key services to community groups and municipalities including:

- Community forestry planning assistance for tree boards and other groups
- Community tree inventory and ordinance assistance
- Arborist/green industry training and certification
- Green industry training and education in tree planting and care
- Pest identification and control recommendations for homeowners and professionals
- Disaster/tornado "releaf" assistance for impacted communities
- Cost-share assistance for community forest design, implementation, management and care

North Dakota

In North Dakota, the state Forest Service offers urban forestry support by providing information, technical assistance, and grants to communities and local governments for planting, protecting, and maintaining trees in urban environments. The Forest Service also provides assistance in developing management plans, inventories, and ordinances or policies, as well as conducting resource assessments.

The North Dakota Community Forestry Council, an advisory group to the State Forester, provides program guidance and maintains priorities, including plant health care, species diversity, right tree-right place, sustainable forestry, and promoting professionalism. The staff is responsible for coordinating statewide Tree City USA programs. They also help communities obtain grants via a variety of programs, including Community Transportation Enhancement, Storm Tree Replacement, Community "Family Forest", and America the Beautiful Program Development and Tree Planting.

South Dakota

The South Dakota Department of Agriculture, Division of Resource Conservation and Forestry has community foresters dedicated to assisting communities cultivate and improve their urban forest. This objective is accomplished through technical assistance, education and training, resource development, and public awareness. The Urban and Community Forestry Program also administers programs in South Dakota, such as Community Forestry Challenge Grant, Tree City USA, Arbor Day Poster Contest, Big Tree Registry, Arborist Training, and the Great Faces, Green Spaces Newsletter. Each year, communities in South Dakota spend upwards of $2.00 per capita maintaining their urban trees.

Table 16.—Species[a] sampled in the urban forest, Kansas, 2008

Genus	Species	Common Name	Number of Trees	Pop %	Leaf Area %	IV[b]	Median d.b.h. (in)	Avg. d.b.h. (in)	Basal Area (ft²)	Structural Value ($ millions)
Acer	negundo	Boxelder	504,250	1.5	1.5	3.0	5.9	7.8	307,734	202.1
Acer	saccharinum	Silver maple	511,650	1.5	3.0	4.5	7.9	13.7	997,917	527.1
Acer	species	Maple	2,243,730	6.8	3.9	10.7	2.1	3.6	371,604	513.7
Betula	species	Birch	1,474,620	4.4	2.1	6.5	2.3	2.8	122,585	167.1
Celtis	species	Hackberry	3,344,320	10.1	14.3	24.4	4.4	5.7	1,305,338	2,235.8
Elaeagnus	angustifolia	Russian olive	29,030	0.1	0.1	0.2	8.5	8.5	12,825	15.4
Fraxinus	species	Ash	1,577,350	4.8	4.7	9.5	4.2	6.3	799,968	1,305.8
Gleditsia	triacanthos	Honeylocust	877,280	2.6	1.4	4.0	6.3	7.6	467,138	404.6
Hardwood	species	Hardwood	3,515,130	10.6	10.0	20.6	3.6	5.3	1,146,523	1,451.8
Juglans	species	Walnut	1,812,710	5.5	10.0	15.5	4.6	8.0	1,392,640	1,331.2
Juniperus	species	Juniper	2,655,330	8.0	6.7	14.7	2.7	4.3	599,401	906.3
Maclura	pomifera	Osage orange	1,700,100	5.1	4.4	9.5	4.2	6.1	716,521	677.5
Malus	sylvestris	Apple	566,240	1.7	1.4	3.1	6.3	7.7	310,884	283.8
Morus	species	Mulberry	958,330	2.9	1.6	4.5	3.3	4.2	182,786	229.3
Picea	species	Spruce	187,200	0.6	0.3	0.9	5.0	4.9	35,862	69.8
Pinus	ponderosa	Ponderosa pine	95,080	0.3	0.0	0.3	5.5	5.2	20,969	32.2
Pinus	species	Pine	30,970	0.1	0.1	0.2	22.5	22.5	89,342	115.3
Pinus	sylvestris	Scotch pine	276,360	0.8	0.7	1.5	6.5	7.8	153,155	374.8
Populus	deltoides	Eastern cottonwood	669,360	2.0	3.8	5.8	7.7	8.9	459,226	271.6
Prunus	species	Cherry	430,660	1.3	1.5	2.8	7.0	8.6	251,061	324.9
Quercus	alba	White oak	1,540,400	4.6	3.9	8.5	7.5	8.4	913,548	1,395.3
Quercus	rubra	Northern red oak	1,017,510	3.1	4.0	7.1	6.5	9.6	953,127	1,528.3
Salix	species	Willow	417,340	1.3	1.0	2.3	5.6	8.5	384,353	271.9
Softwood	species	Softwood	95,080	0.3	0.9	1.2	16.5	17.3	179,539	311.4
Ulmus	pumila	Siberian elm	1,512,990	4.6	3.6	8.2	3.7	8.4	1,588,876	744.6
Ulmus	species	Elm	5,098,150	15.4	14.9	30.3	4.2	6.1	2,132,267	2,452.1

[a] Species refers to tree species, genera, or species groups that were classified during field data collection
[b] IV = importance value (% population + % leaf area)

Tree Species Distribution in Kansas

The species distributions for each land use are illustrated for the 20 most common species or all species if there are less than twenty species in the land-use category. More detailed information on species by land use can be found at: http://nrs.fs.fed.us/data/urban.

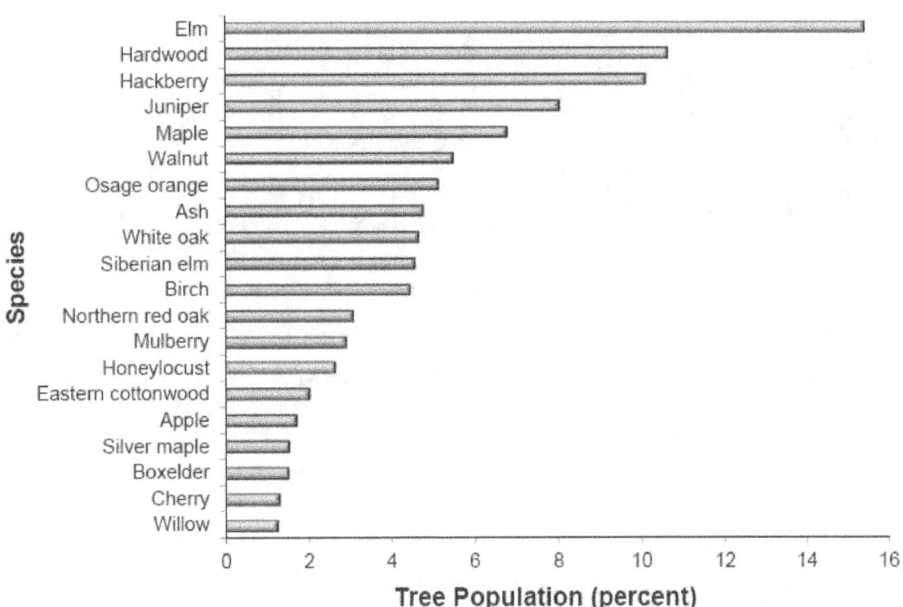

Figure 45.—The 20 most common tree species as a percent of the total urban tree population, Kansas, 2008.

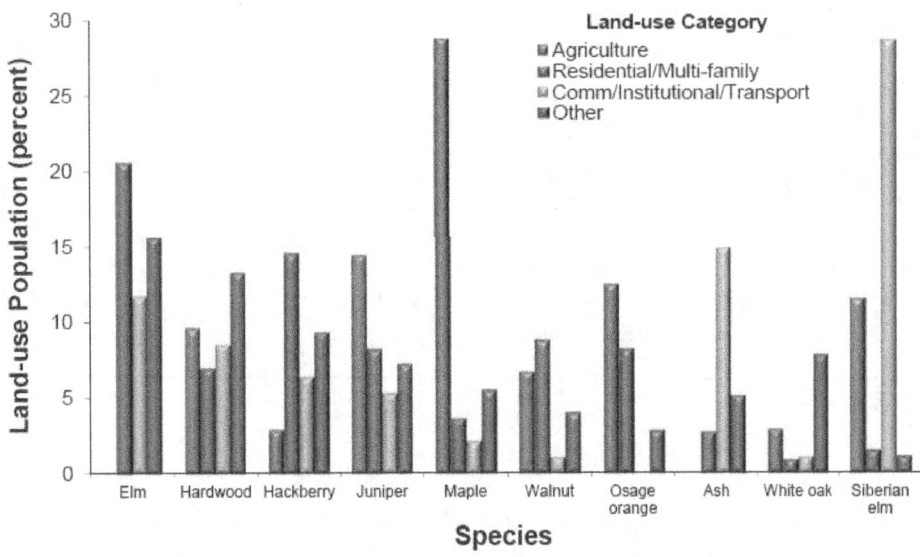

Figure 46.—The percent land-use population occupied by the 10 most common tree species, Kansas, 2008.

For example, elm comprises 20.6 percent of the Residential/Multi-family tree population.

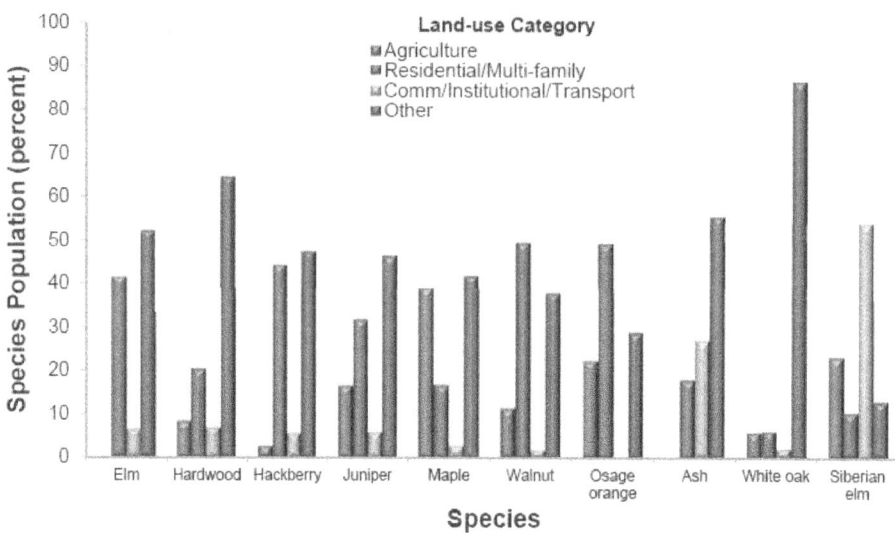

Figure 47.—The percent of species population in each land-use category, Kansas, 2008. For example, 41.3 percent of elm are found within Residential/Multi-family land use.

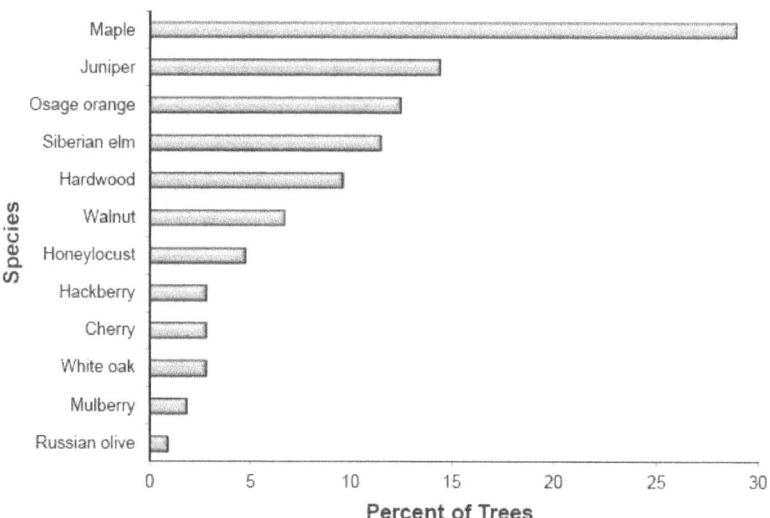

Figure 48.—Percent of trees in Agriculture land use, Kansas, 2008.

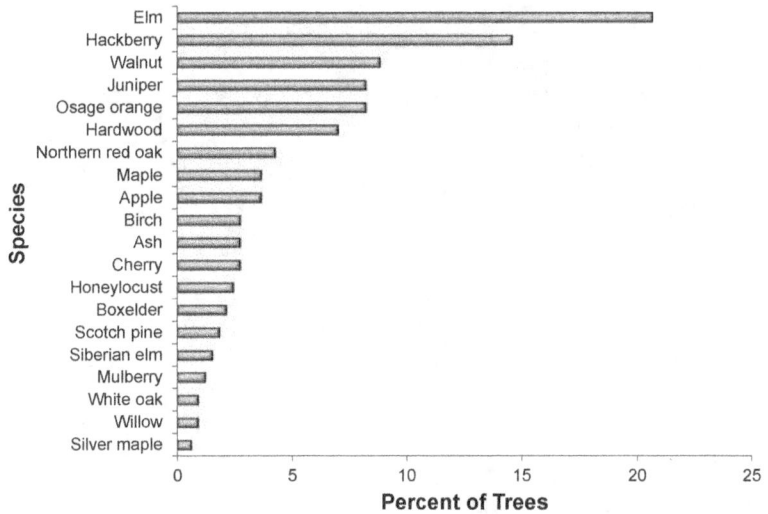

Figure 49.—Percent of trees in Residential/Multi-family land use for 20 most common species, Kansas, 2008.

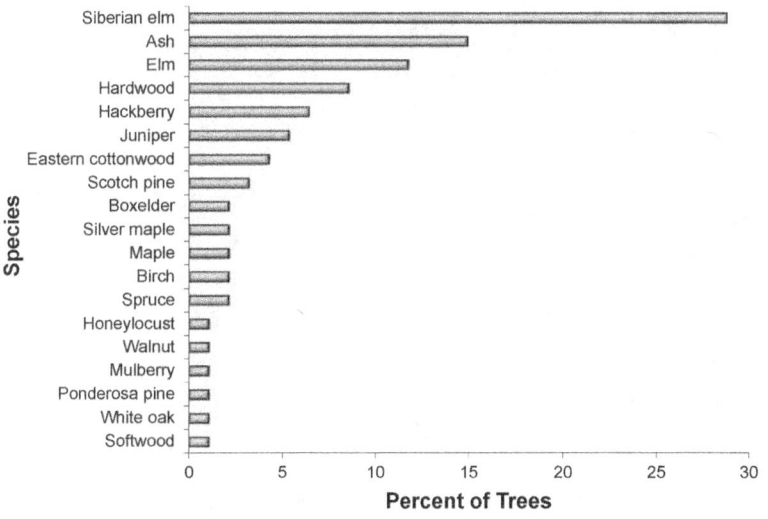

Figure 50.—Percent of trees in Commercial/Institutional/Transportation land use, Kansas, 2008.

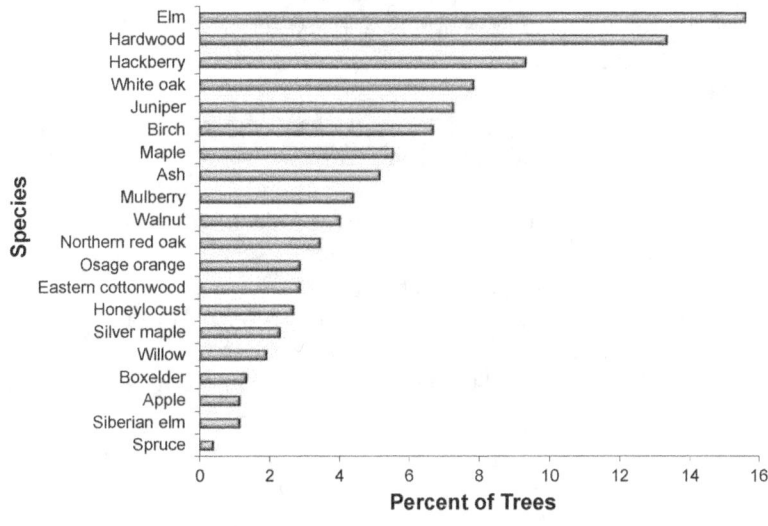

Figure 51.—Percent of trees in Other land use for 20 most common species, Kansas, 2008.

Relative Tree Effects in Kansas

The urban forest in Kansas provides benefits that include carbon storage and sequestration and air pollutant removal. To estimate a relative value of these benefits, tree benefits were compared to estimates of average carbon emissions in the study area[25], average passenger automobile emissions[26], and average household emissions.[27]

General tree information:

Average tree diameter (d.b.h.) = 6.3 in.

Median tree diameter (d.b.h.) = 4.1 in.

Number of trees sampled = 1,043

Number of species sampled = 26

Table 17.—Average tree effects by tree diameter class (d.b.h.), Kansas, 2008

d.b.h. (inch)	Carbon storage			Carbon sequestration			Pollution removal	
	(lbs)	($)	(miles)[a]	(lbs/yr)	($/yr)	(miles)[a]	(lbs)	($)
1-3	8	0.08	30	1.4	0.01	5	0.16	0.61
3-6	43	0.45	160	5.2	0.05	19	0.3	1.04
6-9	140	1.45	510	10.3	0.11	38	0.4	1.49
9-12	313	3.24	1,150	16.1	0.17	59	0.5	1.85
12-15	547	5.66	2,000	23.1	0.24	85	0.8	2.90
15-18	881	9.12	3,230	29.4	0.30	108	0.8	3.12
18-21	1,273	13.17	4,660	39.4	0.41	144	1.4	5.46
21-24	1,616	16.71	5,920	45.7	0.47	168	0.8	3.02
24-27	2,421	25.04	8,870	60.5	0.63	222	1.5	5.51
27-30	3,095	32.02	11,340	63.1	0.65	231	1.1	4.15
30+	5,223	54.03	19,130	107.4	1.11	393	2.5	9.54

[a] miles = number of automobile miles driven that produces emissions equivalent to tree effect

The trees in Kansas provide:

Carbon storage equivalent to:
Amount of carbon (C) emitted in city in 95 days or
Annual carbon emissions from 2,666,000 automobiles or
Annual C emissions from 1,338,500 single family houses

Carbon monoxide removal equivalent to:
Annual carbon monoxide emissions from 473 automobiles or
Annual carbon monoxide emissions from 2,000 family houses

Nitrogen dioxide removal equivalent to:
Annual nitrogen dioxide emissions from 24,100 automobiles or
Annual nitrogen dioxide emissions from 16,100 single family houses

Sulfur dioxide removal equivalent to:
Annual sulfur dioxide emissions from 596,300 automobiles or
Annual sulfur dioxide emissions from 10,000 single family houses

Particulate matter less than 10 micron (PM10) removal equivalent to:
Annual PM10 emissions from 4,557,600 automobiles or
Annual PM10 emissions 440,000 single family houses

Annual C sequestration equivalent to:
Amount of C emitted in city in 3.6 days or
Annual C emissions from 101,800 automobiles or
Annual C emissions from 51,100 single family homes

Appendix III. Urban Tree Species, Distribution, and Effects, Nebraska

Table 18.—Species[a] sampled in the urban forest, Nebraska, 2008

Genus	Species	Common Name	Number of Trees	Pop %	Leaf Area %	IV[b]	Median d.b.h. (in)	Avg. d.b.h. (in)	Basal Area (ft²)	Structural Value ($ millions)
Acer	negundo	Boxelder	155,020	1.2	0.4	1.6	2.5	5.1	43,581	33.8
Acer	saccharinum	Silver maple	211,390	1.6	5.5	7.1	24.5	22.1	783,835	499.0
Acer	species	Maple	225,480	1.7	2.0	3.7	3.5	5.7	91,851	134.2
Betula	species	Birch	98,650	0.7	0.7	1.4	1.7	3.8	22,464	34.0
Celtis	species	Hackberry	1,987,040	14.9	19.2	34.1	4.2	6.6	1,086,439	1,841.3
Elaeagnus	angustifolia	Russian olive	14,090	0.1	0.0	0.1	17.5	17.5	24,903	4.5
Fraxinus	species	Ash	986,470	7.4	6.6	14.0	4.0	6.6	543,691	823.9
Gleditsia	triacanthos	Honeylocust	183,200	1.4	1.3	2.7	12.5	11.4	198,459	284.7
Hardwood	species	Hardwood	944,200	7.1	5.3	12.4	3.1	5.3	309,870	432.3
Juglans	species	Walnut	465,050	3.5	4.2	7.7	3.8	5.3	131,051	192.8
Juniperus	species	Juniper	1,423,340	10.7	7.3	18.0	4.9	5.5	381,842	384.8
Maclura	pomifera	Osage orange	42,280	0.3	0.7	1.0	8.5	8.8	21,060	30.7
Malus	sylvestris	Apple	281,850	2.1	1.2	3.3	3.4	4.8	79,405	104.9
Morus	species	Mulberry	1,677,010	12.6	5.7	18.3	2.4	4.0	326,294	424.1
Picea	species	Spruce	521,420	3.9	3.7	7.6	8.3	8.1	314,405	624.8
Pinus	ponderosa	Ponderosa pine	14,090	0.1	0.2	0.3	11.5	11.5	11,068	17.3
Pinus	species	Pine	126,830	1.0	1.3	2.3	10.5	10.6	118,215	160.5
Pinus	sylvestris	Scotch pine	295,940	2.2	3.3	5.5	10.7	11.3	244,216	401.8
Populus	deltoides	Eastern cottonwood	253,670	1.9	4.3	6.2	11.0	13.6	432,549	315.8
Prunus	species	Cherry	183,200	1.4	1.1	2.5	6.2	7.1	82,014	97.5
Quercus	alba	White oak	253,670	1.9	3.6	5.5	11.0	17.1	719,006	1,451.1
Quercus	rubra	Northern red oak	155,020	1.2	1.5	2.7	7.5	7.7	79,013	145.2
Salix	species	Willow	28,190	0.2	0.3	0.5	6.0	11.5	27,670	16.4
Softwood	species	Softwood	14,090	0.1	0.1	0.2	9.5	9.5	7,686	15.1
Tilia	americana	American basswood	112,740	0.8	2.7	3.5	17.0	18.1	291,230	419.1
Ulmus	pumila	Siberian elm	1,521,990	11.4	10.1	21.5	4.0	6.1	648,273	447.2
Ulmus	species	Elm	1,141,490	8.6	7.5	16.1	3.3	5.0	342,739	424.0

[a] Species refers to tree species, genera, or species groups that were classified during field data collection
[b] IV = importance value (% population + % leaf area)

Tree Species Distribution in Nebraska

The species distributions for each land use are illustrated for the 20 most common species or all species if there are less than twenty species in the land-use category. More detailed information on species by land use can be found at: http://nrs.fs.fed.us/data/urban.

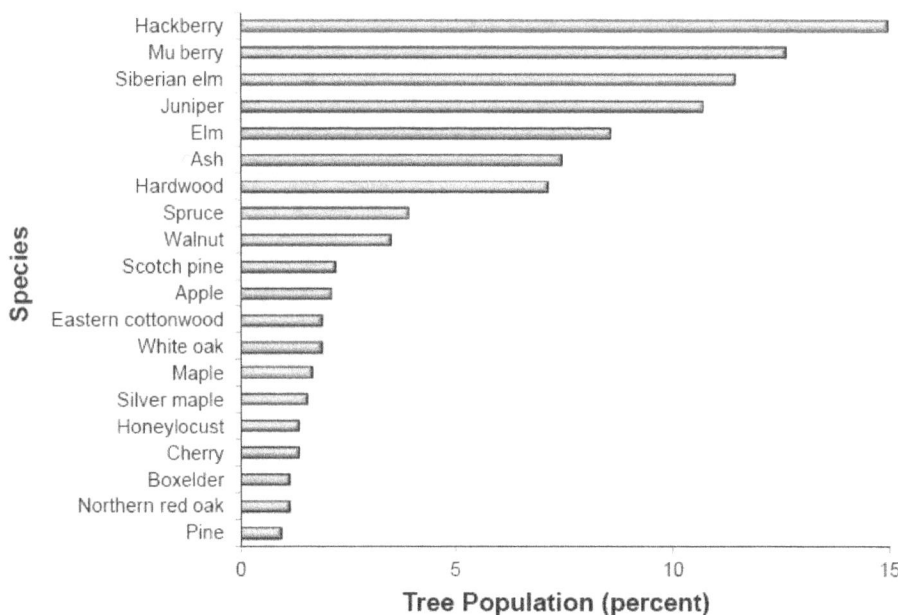

Figure 52.—The 20 most common tree species as a percent of the total urban tree population, Nebraska, 2008.

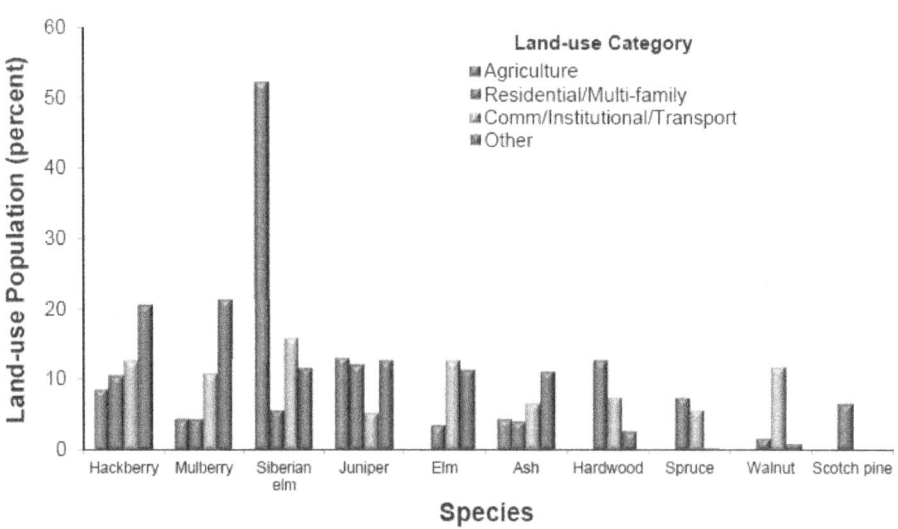

Figure 53.—The percent land-use population occupied by the 10 most common tree species, Nebraska, 2008.

For example, hackberry comprises 12.6 percent of the Commercial/Institutional/ Transportation tree population.

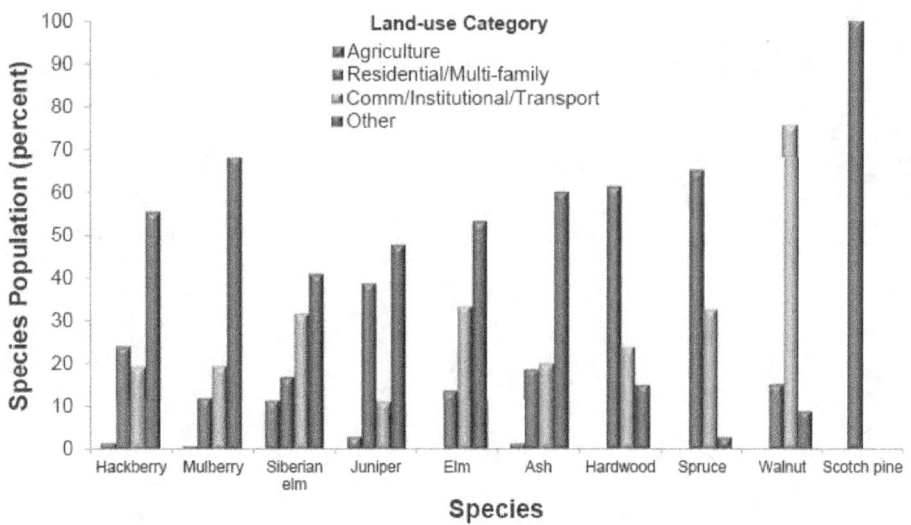

Figure 54.—The percent of species population in each land-use category, Nebraska, 2008. For example, 24.1 percent of hackberry are found within Residential/Multi-family land use.

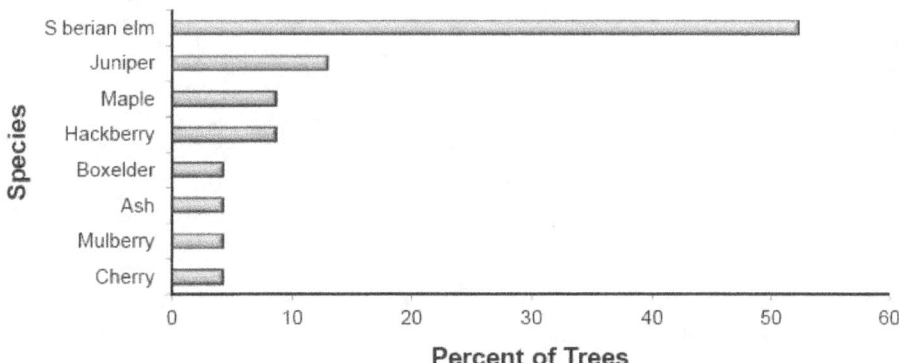

Figure 55.—Percent of trees in Agriculture land use, Nebraska, 2008.

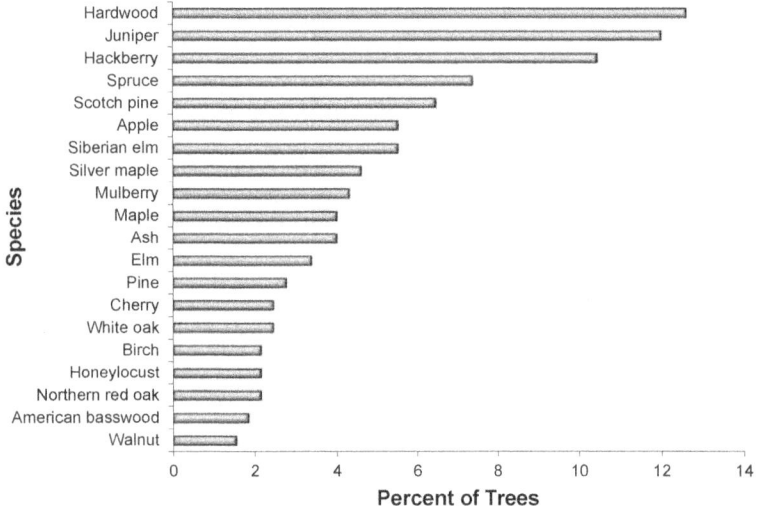

Figure 56.—Percent of trees in Residential/Multi-family land use for 20 most common species, Nebraska, 2008.

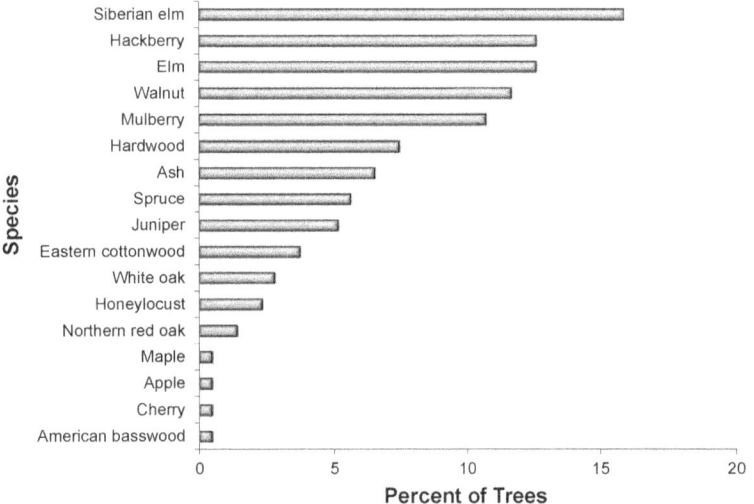

Figure 57.—Percent of trees in Commercial/Institutional/Transportation land use, Nebraska, 2008.

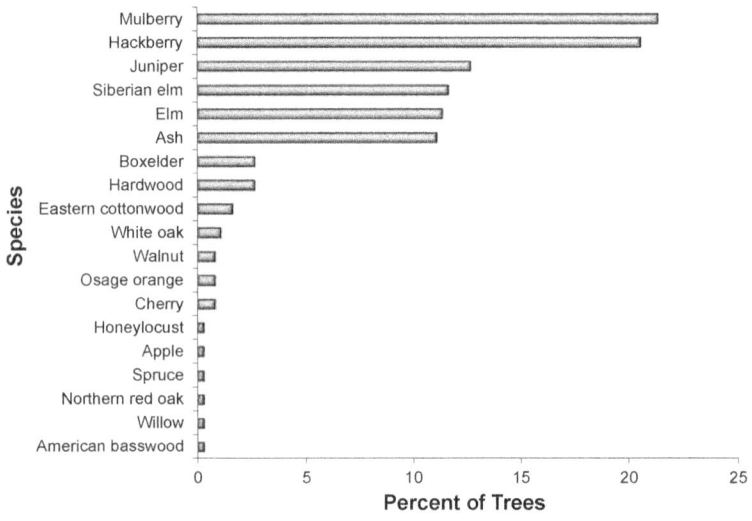

Figure 58.—Percent of trees in Other land use, Nebraska, 2008.

Relative Tree Effects in Nebraska

The urban forest in Nebraska provides benefits that include carbon storage and sequestration and air pollutant removal. To estimate a relative value of these benefits, tree benefits were compared to estimates of average carbon emissions in the study area[25], average passenger automobile emissions[26], and average household emissions.[27]

General tree information:

Average tree diameter (d.b.h.) = 6.7 in.

Median tree diameter (d.b.h.) = 4.2 in.

Number of trees sampled = 941

Number of species sampled = 27

Table 19.—Average tree effects by tree diameter class (d.b.h.), Nebraska, 2008

d.b.h. (inch)	Carbon storage			Carbon sequestration			Pollution removal	
	(lbs)	($)	(miles)[a]	(lbs/yr)	($/yr)	(miles)[a]	(lbs)	($)
1-3	8	0.08	30	2.0	0.02	8	0.20	0.68
3-6	47	0.49	170	6.9	0.07	25	0.5	1.83
6-9	150	1.55	550	12.1	0.13	44	1.1	3.81
9-12	298	3.09	1,090	19.4	0.20	71	1.9	6.50
12-15	524	5.43	1,920	24.0	0.25	88	1.9	6.67
15-18	824	8.53	3,020	31.1	0.32	114	2.3	8.15
18-21	1,296	13.41	4,750	45.1	0.47	165	3.5	12.04
21-24	1,741	18.01	6,380	48.2	0.50	177	3.7	12.75
24-27	2,197	22.73	8,050	59.4	0.61	218	5.4	18.65
27-30	3,484	36.04	12,760	88.2	0.91	323	5.0	17.51
30+	5,084	52.59	18,620	92.0	0.95	337	5.6	19.51

[a] miles = number of automobile miles driven that produces emissions equivalent to tree effect

The trees in Nebraska provide:

Carbon storage equivalent to:
Amount of carbon (C) emitted in city in 70 days or
Annual carbon emissions from 1,258,000 automobiles or
Annual C emissions from 631,700 single family houses

Carbon monoxide removal equivalent to:
Annual carbon monoxide emissions from 174 automobiles or
Annual carbon monoxide emissions from 700 family houses

Nitrogen dioxide removal equivalent to:
Annual nitrogen dioxide emissions from 13,100 automobiles or
Annual nitrogen dioxide emissions from 8,700 single family houses

Sulfur dioxide removal equivalent to:
Annual sulfur dioxide emissions from 273,500 automobiles or
Annual sulfur dioxide emissions from 4,600 single family houses

Particulate matter less than 10 micron (PM10) removal equivalent to:
Annual PM10 emissions from 10,660,600 automobiles or
Annual PM10 emissions 1,029,100 single family houses

Annual C sequestration equivalent to:
Amount of C emitted in city in 2.8 days or
Annual C emissions from 50,700 automobiles or
Annual C emissions from 25,500 single family homes

Table 20.—Species[a] sampled in the urban forest, North Dakota, 2008-2009

Genus	Species	Common Name	Number of Trees	Pop %	Leaf Area %	IV[b]	Median d.b.h. (in)	Avg. d.b.h. (in)	Basal Area (ft²)	Structural Value ($ millions)
Acer	negundo	Boxelder	83,460	8.6	5.4	14.0	9.0	9.9	75,382	61.8
Acer	saccharinum	Silver maple	10,430	1.1	3.8	4.9	29.0	35.0	72,068	72.2
Acer	species	Maple	26,080	2.7	0.8	3.5	3.8	3.9	2,902	10.0
Betula	species	Birch	5,220	0.5	0.2	0.7	19.5	19.5	11,380	26.3
Celtis	species	Hackberry	5,220	0.5	0.3	0.8	6.5	6.5	1,394	4.8
Elaeagnus	angustifolia	Russian olive	15,650	1.6	1.3	2.9	5.5	7.5	6,543	13.7
Fraxinus	species	Ash	375,580	38.5	27.2	65.7	8.2	8.3	203,761	463.5
Juglans	species	Walnut	5,220	0.5	0.8	1.3	11.5	11.5	4,097	9.7
Juniperus	species	Juniper	15,650	1.6	0.4	2.0	3.5	3.8	1,735	4.1
Malus	sylvestris	Apple	52,160	5.3	1.6	6.9	7.3	6.7	16,103	44.7
Picea	species	Spruce	130,410	13.4	20.5	33.9	8.2	8.4	66,665	174.9
Pinus	ponderosa	Ponderosa pine	20,870	2.1	2.5	4.6	7.0	10.5	17,185	23.8
Populus	deltoides	Eastern cottonwood	78,250	8.0	18.4	26.4	23.2	23.1	269,626	217.6
Prunus	species	Cherry	5,220	0.5	0.0	0.5	1.5	1.5	114	0.1
Quercus	alba	White oak	10,430	1.1	0.1	1.2	12.0	13.0	10,499	23.8
Salix	species	Willow	10,430	1.1	2.4	3.5	12.0	14.5	13,315	9.5
Tilia	americana	American basswood	10,430	1.1	0.1	1.2	0.0	1.2	142	0.8
Ulmus	pumila	Siberian elm	52,160	5.3	2.5	7.8	3.3	6.2	21,652	11.0
Ulmus	species	Elm	62,600	6.4	11.8	18.2	14.0	15.3	97,103	173.3

[a] Species refers to tree species, genera, or species groups that were classified during field data collection

[b] IV = importance value (% population + % leaf area)

Tree Species Distribution in North Dakota

The species distributions for each land use are illustrated for the 20 most common species or all species if there are less than twenty species in the land-use category. More detailed information on species by land use can be found at: http://nrs.fs.fed.us/data/urban.

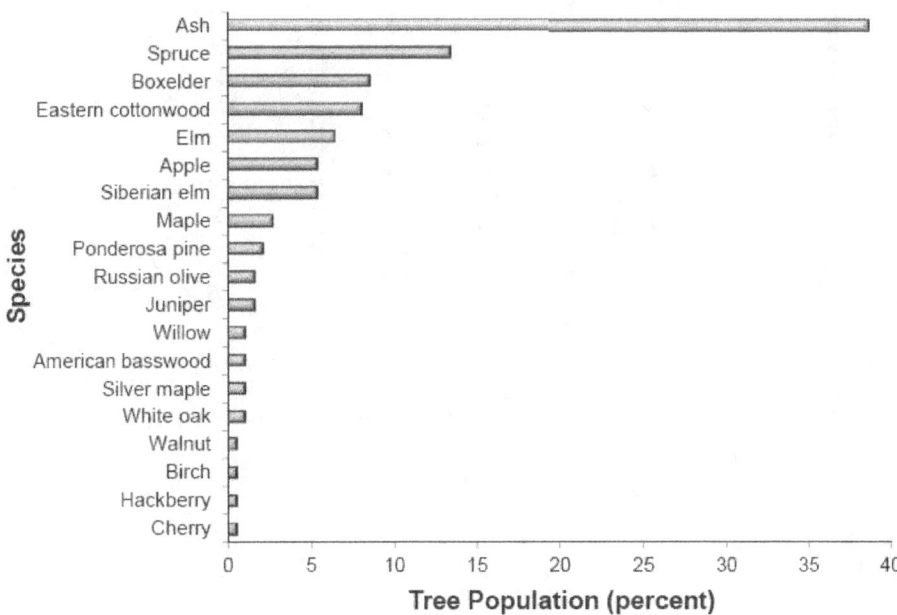

Figure 59.—The 20 most common tree species as a percent of the total urban tree population, North Dakota, 2008-2009.

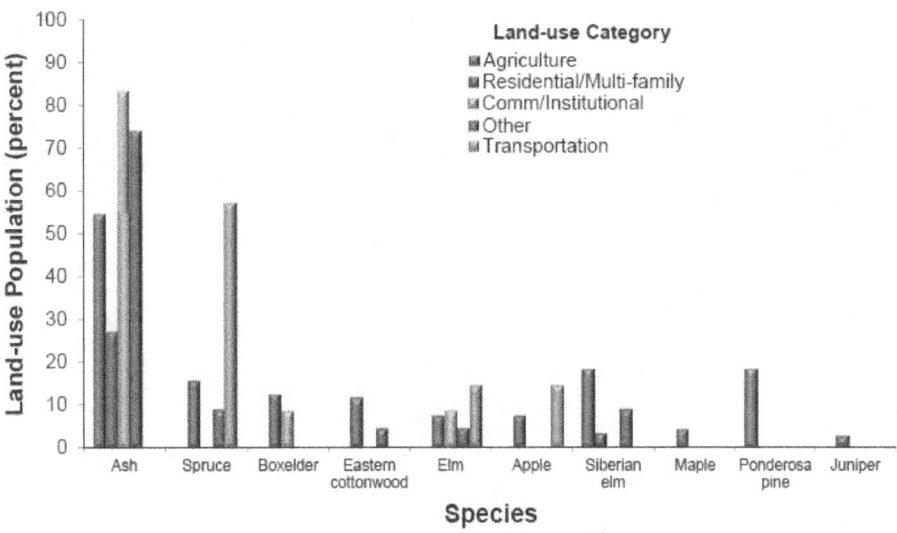

Figure 60.—The percent land-use population occupied by the 10 most common tree species, North Dakota, 2008-2009.

For example, ash comprises 83.3 percent of the Commercial/Institutional tree population.

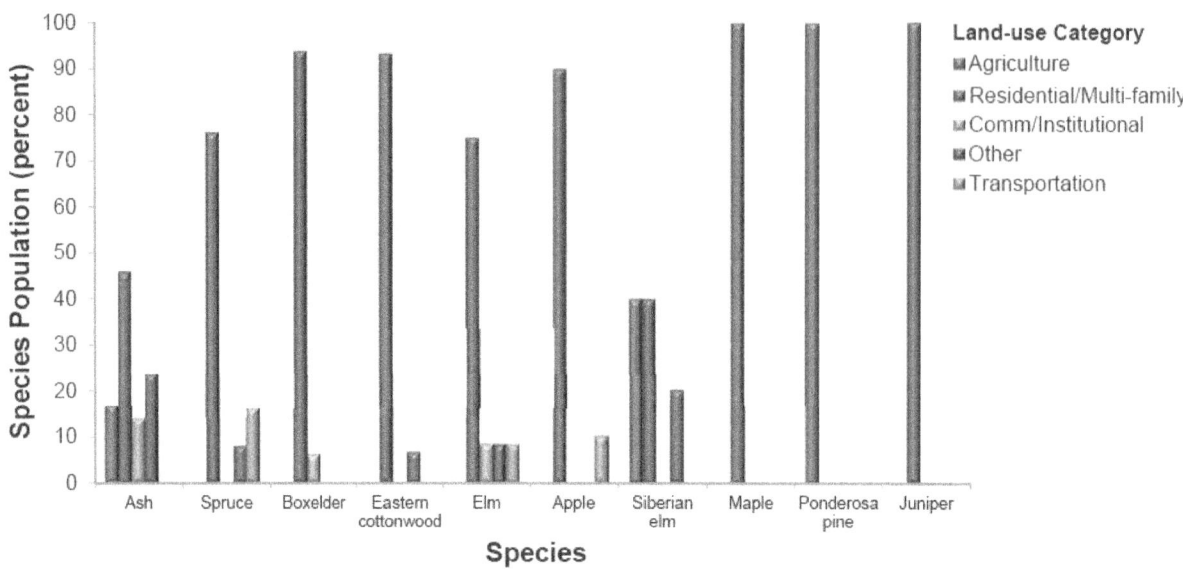

Figure 61.—The percent of species population in each land-use category, North Dakota, 2008-2009.

For example, 45.8 percent of ash are found within Residential/Multi-family land use.

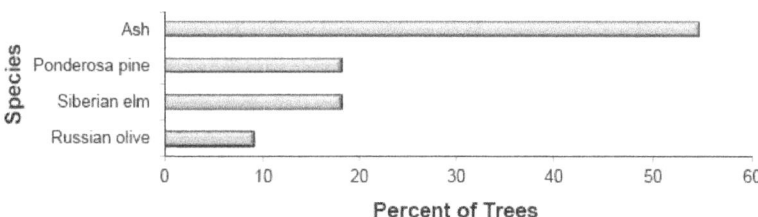

Figure 62.—Percent of trees in Agriculture land use, North Dakota, 2008-2009.

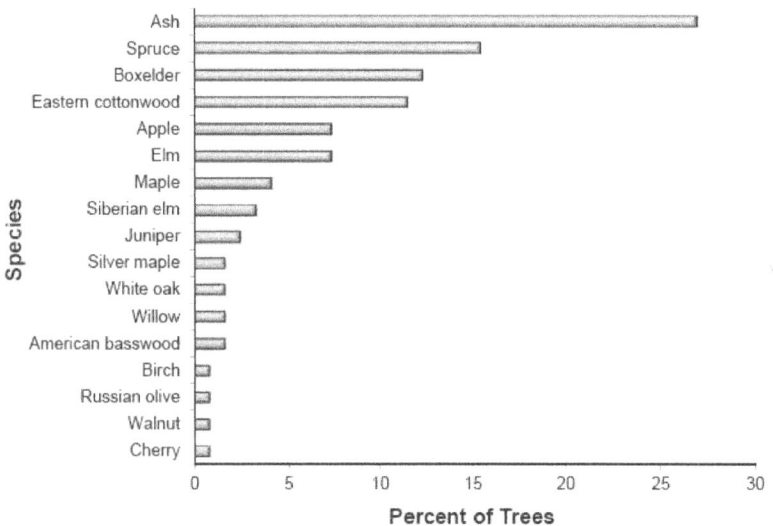

Figure 63.—Percent of trees in Residential/Multi-family land use, North Dakota, 2008-2009.

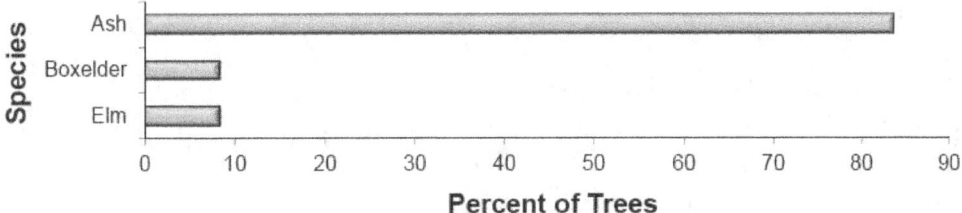

Figure 64.—Percent of trees in Commercial/Institutional land use, North Dakota, 2008-2009.

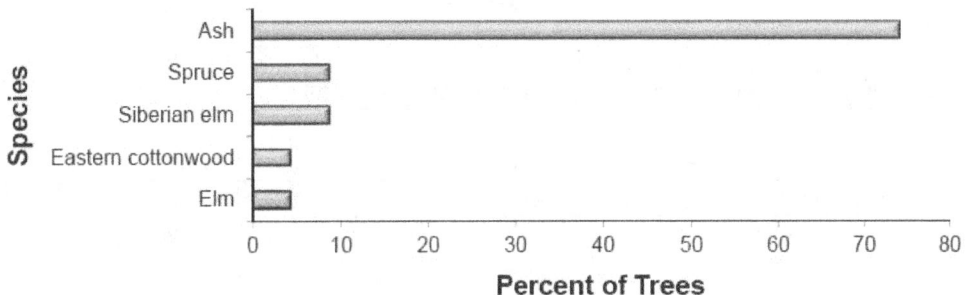

Figure 65.—Percent of trees in Other land use, North Dakota, 2008-2009.

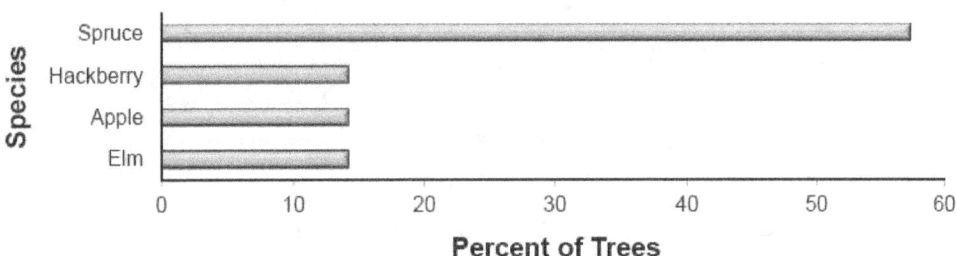

Figure 66.—Percent of trees in Transportation land use, North Dakota, 2008-2009.

Relative Tree Effects in North Dakota

The urban forest in North Dakota provides benefits that include carbon storage and sequestration and air pollutant removal. To estimate a relative value of these benefits, tree benefits were compared to estimates of average carbon emissions in the study area[25], average passenger automobile emissions[26], and average household emissions.[27]

General tree information:

Average tree diameter (d.b.h.) = 10.1 in.

Median tree diameter (d.b.h.) = 8.5 in.

Number of trees sampled = 186

Number of species sampled = 19

Table 21.—Average tree effects by tree diameter class (d.b.h.), North Dakota, 2008-2009

d.b.h. (inch)	Carbon storage			Carbon sequestration			Pollution removal	
	(lbs)	($)	(miles)[a]	(lbs/yr)	($/yr)	(miles)[a]	(lbs)	($)
1-3	12	0.12	40	2.6	0.03	9	0.1	0.26
3-6	53	0.55	190	7.6	0.08	28	0.1	0.38
6-9	154	1.59	560	13.1	0.14	48	0.2	0.85
9-12	314	3.25	1,150	18.4	0.19	67	0.4	1.36
12-15	525	5.43	1,920	23.5	0.24	86	0.4	1.64
15-18	865	8.95	3,170	29.0	0.30	106	0.7	2.61
18-21	1,238	12.81	4,540	41.4	0.43	152	0.6	2.44
21-24	1,677	17.35	6,140	38.7	0.40	142	0.5	1.94
24-27	2,275	23.54	8,330	46.7	0.48	171	0.8	3.05
27-30	2,955	30.57	10,820	59.1	0.61	216	1.3	5.10
30+	5,473	56.62	20,040	93.3	0.97	342	1.0	3.81

[a] miles = number of automobile miles driven that produces emissions equivalent to tree effect

The trees in North Dakota provide:

Carbon storage equivalent to:
Amount of carbon (C) emitted in city in 23 days or
Annual carbon emissions from 146,000 automobiles or
Annual C emissions from 73,400 single family houses

Carbon monoxide removal equivalent to:
Annual carbon monoxide emissions from 20 automobiles or
Annual carbon monoxide emissions from 100 family houses

Nitrogen dioxide removal equivalent to:
Annual nitrogen dioxide emissions from 300 automobiles or
Annual nitrogen dioxide emissions from 200 single family houses

Sulfur dioxide removal equivalent to:
Annual sulfur dioxide emissions from 18,100 automobiles or
Annual sulfur dioxide emissions from 300 single family houses

Particulate matter less than 10 micron (PM10) removal equivalent to:
Annual PM10 emissions from 78,600 automobiles or
Annual PM10 emissions 7,600 single family houses

Annual C sequestration equivalent to:
Amount of C emitted in city in 0.8 days or
Annual C emissions from 5,300 automobiles or
Annual C emissions from 2,700 single family homes

Appendix V. Urban Tree Species, Distribution, and Effects, South Dakota

Table 22.—Species[a] sampled in the urban forest, South Dakota, 2008

Genus	Species	Common Name	Number of Trees	Pop %	Leaf Area %	IV[b]	Median d.b.h. (in)	Avg d.b.h. (in)	Basal Area (ft²)	Structural Value ($ millions)
Acer	negundo	Boxelder	274,900	5.1	3.9	9.0	7.4	7.3	112,346	72.6
Acer	saccharinum	Silver maple	8,870	0.2	0.6	0.8	13.5	13.5	9,480	9.1
Acer	species	Maple	141,540	2.6	7.8	10.4	8.0	12.4	193,442	509.9
Betula	species	Birch	8,870	0.2	0.0	0.2	5.5	5.5	1,741	2.1
Celtis	species	Hackberry	8,870	0.2	0.0	0.2	1.5	1.5	193	0.7
Elaeagnus	angustifolia	Russian olive	26,600	0.5	0.3	0.8	1.5	2.9	2,612	3.5
Fraxinus	species	Ash	1,104,310	20.4	26.5	46.9	6.9	8.2	707,760	1,650.3
Gleditsia	triacanthos	Honeylocust	131,630	2.4	2.2	4.6	12.3	9.7	113,992	215.5
Hardwood	species	Hardwood	124,150	2.3	2.0	4.3	3.0	6.6	71,776	131.6
Juglans	species	Walnut	35,470	0.7	1.7	2.4	6.0	8.3	25,489	33.9
Juniperus	species	Juniper	53,210	1.0	0.6	1.6	4.7	5.7	16,299	35.3
Malus	sylvestris	Apple	70,600	1.3	0.7	2.0	4.0	4.9	14,050	32.9
Morus	species	Mulberry	70,940	1.3	0.6	1.9	3.5	4.0	9,867	15.5
Picea	species	Spruce	124,150	2.3	2.7	5.0	7.4	7.9	71,673	183.0
Pinus	ponderosa	Ponderosa pine	1,152,120	21.3	15.2	36.5	5.0	6.2	454,993	885.7
Pinus	species	Pine	449,830	8.3	2.9	11.2	7.5	7.1	164,020	167.5
Pinus	sylvestris	Scotch pine	26,600	0.5	0.2	0.7	4.5	3.6	2,999	2.6
Populus	deltoides	Eastern cottonwood	123,800	2.3	7.2	9.5	13.5	15.1	275,373	346.8
Prunus	species	Cherry	150,060	2.8	2.8	5.6	5.8	6.0	40,388	79.6
Quercus	alba	White oak	248,300	4.6	1.8	6.4	3.0	3.8	33,417	66.6
Salix	species	Willow	505,470	9.3	5.1	14.4	2.7	4.7	123,335	76.2
Softwood	species	Softwood	26,600	0.5	0.0	0.5	0.0	1.4	532	1.0
Sorbus	americana	American mountain ash	17,740	0.3	0.5	0.8	6.0	9.0	9,915	15.2
Tilia	americana	American basswood	44,340	0.8	2.0	2.8	6.5	10.3	36,662	94.3
Ulmus	pumila	Siberian elm	174,920	3.2	2.7	5.9	7.2	6.4	49,281	47.4
Ulmus	species	Elm	310,030	5.7	9.9	15.6	7.2	9.4	249,291	450.6

[a] Species refers to tree species, genera, or species groups that were classified during field data collection
[b] IV = importance value (% population + % leaf area)

Tree Species Distribution in South Dakota

The species distributions for each land use are illustrated for the 20 most common species or all species if there are less than twenty species in the land-use category. More detailed information on species by land use can be found at: http://nrs.fs.fed.us/data/urban.

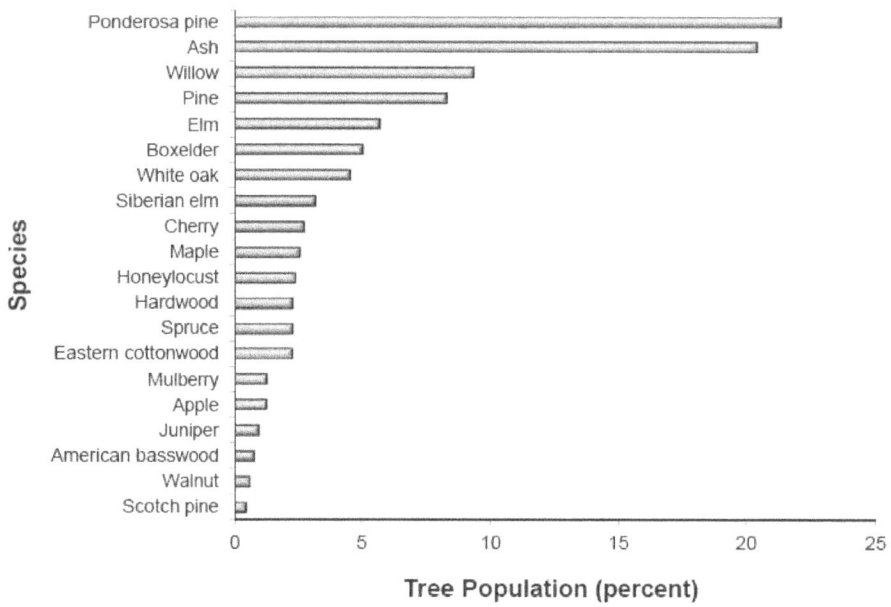

Figure 67.—The 20 most common tree species as a percent of the total urban tree population, South Dakota, 2008.

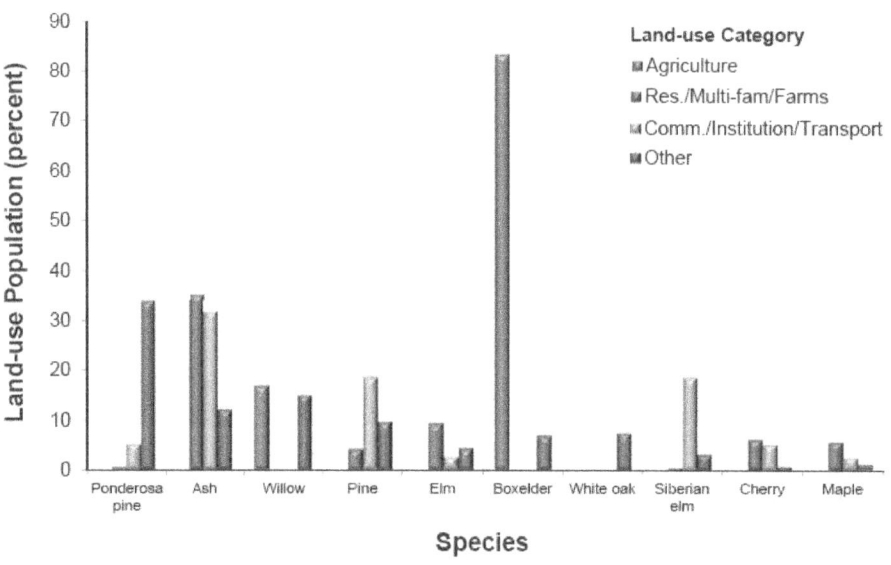

Figure 68.—The percent land-use population occupied by the 10 most common tree species, South Dakota, 2008.

For example, ponderosa pine comprises 34.0 percent of the "other" tree population.

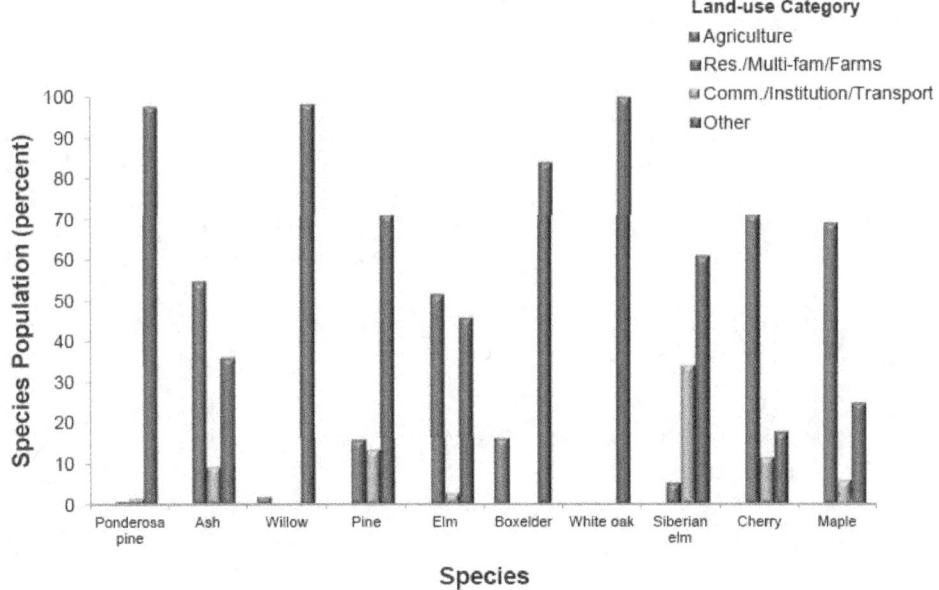

Figure 69.—The percent of species population in each land-use category, South Dakota, 2008.

For example, 97.8 percent of ponderosa pine are found within "other" land use.

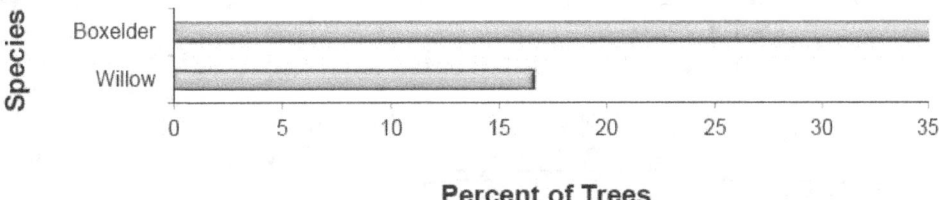

Figure 70.—Percent of trees in Agriculture land use, South Dakota, 2008.

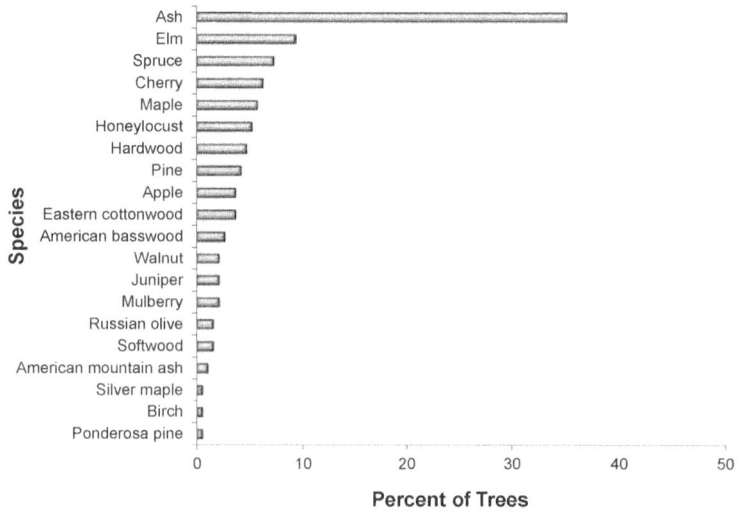

Figure 71.—Percent of trees in Residential/Multi-family/Farms land use, South Dakota, 2008.

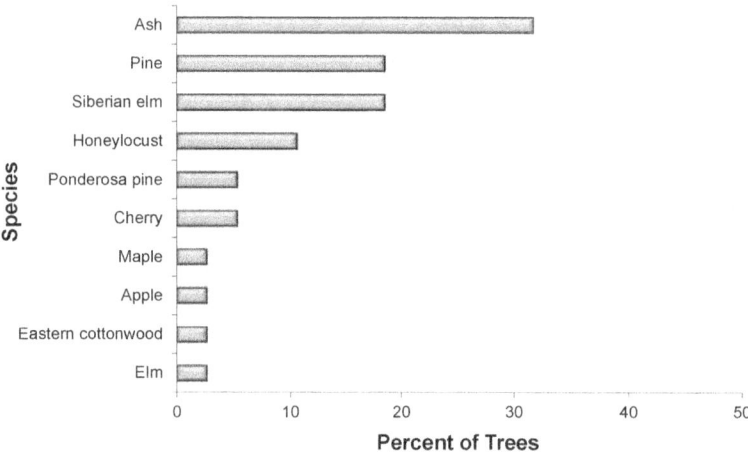

Figure 72.—Percent of trees in Commercial/Institutional/Transportation land use, South Dakota, 2008.

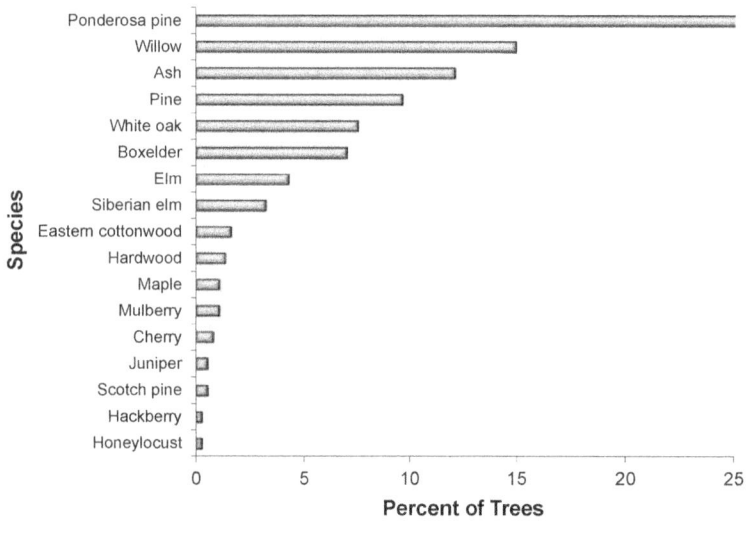

Figure 73. Percent of trees in Other land use, South Dakota, 2008

Relative Tree Effects in South Dakota

The urban forest in South Dakota provides benefits that include carbon storage and sequestration and air pollutant removal. To estimate a relative value of these benefits, tree benefits were compared to estimates of average carbon emissions in the study area[25], average passenger automobile emissions[26], and average household emissions.[27]

General tree information:

Average tree diameter (d.b.h.) = 7.3 in.

Median tree diameter (d.b.h.) = 6.2 in.

Number of trees sampled = 612

Number of species sampled = 26

Table 23.—Average tree effects by tree diameter class (d.b.h.), South Dakota, 2008

d.b.h. (inch)	Carbon storage			Carbon sequestration			Pollution removal	
	(lbs)	($)	(miles)[a]	(lbs/yr)	($/yr)	(miles)[a]	(lbs)	($)
1-3	7	0.07	20	1.4	0.01	5	0.14	0.52
3-6	49	0.50	180	5.6	0.06	20	0.3	0.99
6-9	135	1.40	490	9.3	0.10	34	0.4	1.33
9-12	259	2.68	950	13.7	0.14	50	0.6	2.35
12-15	495	5.12	1,810	19.5	0.20	71	0.8	2.83
15-18	797	8.24	2,920	29.2	0.30	107	1.3	4.69
18-21	1,219	12.62	4,470	35.3	0.37	129	2.2	8.08
21-24	1,764	18.25	6,460	47.2	0.49	173	2.0	7.41
24-27	1,685	17.43	6,170	40.4	0.42	148	1.0	3.79
27-30	3,247	33.59	11,890	70.8	0.73	259	3.9	14.40
30+	6,332	65.51	23,190	106.1	1.10	389	4.1	15.10

[a] miles = number of automobile miles driven that produces emissions equivalent to tree effect

The trees in South Dakota provide:

Carbon storage equivalent to:
Amount of carbon (C) emitted in city in 52 days or
Annual carbon emissions from 418,000 automobiles or
Annual C emissions from 210,100 single family houses

Carbon monoxide removal equivalent to:
Annual carbon monoxide emissions from 135 automobiles or
Annual carbon monoxide emissions from 600 family houses

Nitrogen dioxide removal equivalent to:
Annual nitrogen dioxide emissions from 3,400 automobiles or
Annual nitrogen dioxide emissions from 2,200 single family houses

Sulfur dioxide removal equivalent to:
Annual sulfur dioxide emissions from 138,200 automobiles or
Annual sulfur dioxide emissions from 2,300 single family houses

Particulate matter less than 10 micron (PM10) removal equivalent to:
Annual PM10 emissions from 1,071,000 automobiles or
Annual PM10 emissions 103,400 single family houses

Annual C sequestration equivalent to:
Amount of C emitted in city in 2.1 days or
Annual C emissions from 17,100 automobiles or
Annual C emissions from 8,600 single family homes

Appendix VI. Comparison of State Urban Forests

A commonly asked question is, "How does this state compare to other states?" Although comparison among states should be made with caution as there are many attributes of a state that affect urban forest structure and functions, summary data are provided from other states analyzed using the i-Tree Eco model.

Table 24.—States' urban forest summary data (total for trees)

State	% Tree cover	Number of trees	Carbon storage (tons)	Carbon sequestration (tons/yr)	Pollution removal (tons/yr)[a]	Pollution value ($)[b]
Tennessee[28]	37.7	284,116,000	16,938,000	889,900	27,141	203,886,000
Wisconsin[29]	26.7	130,619,000	6,147,000	400,000	7,057	53,247,000
Indiana[30]	20.0	92,725,000	9,400,000	313,000	7,235	51,929,000
Kansas	14.0	33,141,000	4,441,000	169,600	6,256	47,424,000
Nebraska	15.0	13,317,000	2,096,000	84,500	6,714	46,775,000
South Dakota	17.0	5,414,000	697,000	28,400	1,350	9,965,000
North Dakota	2.7	975,000	243,000	8,800	151	1,149,000

[a] Pollution removal and values are for carbon monoxide, sulfur and nitrogen dioxide, ozone, and particulate matter less than 10 microns (PM10)

[b] Pollution values updated to 2007 values

Table 25.—States' urban forest tree effects (per acre values)

State	No. of trees	Carbon storage (tons)	Carbon sequestration (tons/yr)	Pollution removal (lbs/yr)	Pollution value ($)[a]
Tennessee[28]	182.3	10.9	0.57	34.8	130.8
Wisconsin[29]	145.0	6.8	0.44	15.7	59.1
Indiana[30]	77.6	7.9	0.26	12.1	43.5
Kansas	34.6	4.6	0.18	13.1	49.5
Nebraska	28.3	4.5	0.18	28.6	99.6
South Dakota	18.5	2.4	0.10	9.2	34.1
North Dakota	3.8	0.9	0.03	1.2	4.4

[a] Pollution values updated to 2007 values

Appendix VII. General Recommendations for Air Quality Improvement

Urban vegetation can directly and indirectly affect local and regional air quality by altering the urban atmospheric environment. Four main ways that urban trees affect air quality are:

Temperature reduction and other microclimatic effects
Removal of air pollutants
Emission of volatile organic compounds (VOC) and tree maintenance emissions
Energy conservation on buildings and consequent power plant emissions

The cumulative and interactive effects of trees on climate, pollution removal, and VOC and power plant emissions determine the overall impact of trees on air pollution. Cumulative studies involving urban tree impacts on ozone have revealed that increased urban canopy cover, particularly with low VOC emitting species, leads to reduced ozone concentrations in cities. Local urban forest management decisions also can help improve air quality.

Urban forest management strategies to help improve air quality include:

Strategy	Reason
Increase the number of healthy trees	Increase pollution removal
Sustain existing tree cover	Maintain pollution removal levels
Maximize use of low VOC-emitting trees	Reduces ozone and carbon monoxide formation
Sustain large, healthy trees	Large trees have greatest per-tree effects
Use long-lived trees	Reduce long-term pollutant emissions from planting and removal
Use low maintenance trees	Reduce pollutants emissions from maintenance activities
Reduce fossil fuel use in maintaining vegetation	Reduce pollutant emissions
Plant trees in energy conserving locations	Reduce pollutant emissions from power plants
Plant trees to shade parked cars	Reduce vehicular VOC emissions
Supply ample water to vegetation	Enhance pollution removal and temperature reduction
Plant trees in polluted or heavily populated areas	Maximizes tree air quality benefits
Avoid pollutant-sensitive species	Improve tree health
Utilize evergreen trees for particulate matter	Year-round removal of particles

Nebraska Forest Service